WORLD WAR II IN THE PACIFIC

"Remember Pearl Harbor"

R. Conrad Stein

—American War Series—

Enslow Publishers, Inc.

44 Fadem Road	PO Box 38
Box 699	Aldershot
Springfield, NJ 07081	Hants GU12 6BP
USA	UK

Library of Congress Cataloging-in-Publication Data

Stein, R. Conrad.
    World War II in the Pacific : remember Pearl Harbor / R. Conrad
  Stein.
         p. cm. — (American war series)
       Includes bibliographical references (p.) and index.
       ISBN 0-89490-524-4
       1. World War, 1939-1945—Campaigns—Pacific Area—Juvenile
literature. [1. World War, 1939-1945— Campaigns— Pacific Area.]
I. Title. II. Title: World War Two in the Pacific. III. Series.
D769.S74 1994
940.54'26—dc20   93-33623
                                                    CIP
                                                    AC
Printed in the United States of America

10 9 8 7 6 5 4

Illustration Credits: Courtesy of the Prints and Photographs Division,
Library of Congress, pp. 12, 17, 19, 21, 47, 74, 94, 104; Enslow
Publishers, Inc., pp. 30, 93; National Archives, pp. 9, 10, 14, 15, 26, 35,
39, 40, 42, 44, 48, 56, 59, 61, 63, 72, 76, 79, 81, 85, 92, 95, 100, 102,
106, 108, 111, 113, 114, 115; Courtesy of the Smithsonian Institution, pp.
31, 89.

Cover Illustration: Courtesy of the Prints and Photographs Division,
Library of Congress.

Contents

Foreword

I spent the summer of 1945 at a YMCA boys' camp somewhere in Wisconsin. I was only eight years old and homesick during most of my stay. But I recall having delirious fun on Invasion Day, when we played special war games. Some boys dug foxholes. Others charged at them, just as in a real battle. We used sticks as rifles, and the counselors wore surplus army helmets. It was the height of World War II, and we had grown up watching war movies and reading about heroes in uniform. To us warfare was an adventure.

I joined the U.S. Marine Corps in 1955 at the age of eighteen. I still believed that war was a thrilling experience, a stage on which young men become heroes. But in the Marine Corps I met an officer who had been wounded when he was hit by flying bone fragments that came from his best friend who had been blown to bits by a shell. A grizzled old sergeant wept when he remembered seeing the blackened corpses of two children burned to death by a napalm bomb on Okinawa. Because of my Marine Corps experience I came to see war as a damnable practice, promoted only by madmen.

Despite my hatred of war I retain a powerful interest in World War II. I've read countless books on the subject. I've studied and second-guessed the strategies employed by generals and admirals on both sides. I am a trivia expert on details concerning World War II planes, ships, and tanks. I say this without apology—American history has always fascinated me. World War II was the biggest event of twentieth-century American life. The war shaped millions of lives, including my own.

U.S. Uselessly Extending Talks. Has No
Intention of Compromise with Japan.
—Headlines in the Tokyo newspaper *Asahi Shimbun,*
on December 6, 1941.

"This Is
No Drill!"

It was 6:40 A.M. when the helmsman of the destroyer U.S.S. *Ward* spotted a suspicious object in the waters ahead. The warship was patrolling the mouth of Pearl Harbor, Hawaii, America's largest naval base in the Pacific. Three hours earlier another American ship had reported seeing the periscope of a submarine. Now, in the early morning sunlight, the *Ward*'s captain and all the sailors on deck spotted the conning tower of a half-submerged submarine plowing through the waves. The gunners opened fire, and one scored a direct hit. Although the crew was confused as to the origin and destination of the submarine, they still broke into a cheer. The captain radioed headquarters at Pearl Harbor to report he had sunk an unknown submarine.

It was December 7, 1941. Officers at Pearl Harbor pondered the *Ward*'s radio report. Although war raged in Europe and Asia, the United States was at peace. Consequently, American military leaders felt little sense of urgency. The officers decided to wait for further developments. Besides, it was a Sunday morning, and all the top brass were sleeping late. Surely there was no need to waken generals and admirals.

At 7:00 A.M., two radar operators near Pearl Harbor saw a strange blip on their screens. Radar sets were new and rather mystifying devices in 1941. The two army privates operating the installation had only a few months experience with radar. One of the men, Private George Elliot, telephoned the Pearl Harbor Information Center.

"Sir, there's a huge number of airplanes coming from the north at three degrees east."

Only one officer was working at the Information Center that Sunday morning. He knew that a squadron of American B-17 bombers had taken off from California earlier and was due to land in Hawaii soon. He concluded that the radar operators had sighted the friendly planes.

Bobbing in the waves 200 miles north of Hawaii was a huge Japanese naval fleet led by six aircraft carriers. Before dawn a flight of almost 100 Japanese fighters and bombers roared off six flight decks and headed toward Pearl Harbor. One of the flyers was Lieutenant Yoshio

Shiga, the leader of a fighter group. At 7:50 A.M. he spotted the target. Shiga was astonished. There were no enemy planes in the air. The morning sun revealed a row of battleships below him, all lined up like cars in a parking lot. Shiga banked his plane and dove for the attack. He shouted into his radio the code words that told his superiors the group had achieved complete surprise:

TORA! TORA! TORA!

Serving aboard the battleship U.S.S. *Oklahoma* at Pearl Harbor was Seaman First Class William Fomby. Fomby worked as a cook, and had just finished serving breakfast when he heard the rumbling of airplanes at close range. "I remember I dried my hands on my apron and walked out [on deck] to look." He saw what he thought were American planes practicing bombing runs over the battleships. Then, from his left, came an earth-shaking explosion. One of the planes had dropped a bomb that had blown up on Ford Island, a speck of land in the middle of the harbor. Still believing the planes were American, Fomby said to the man next to him, "Somebody's sure going to catch hell for [accidentally dropping that bomb."][1]

On the fantail of the battleship U.S.S. *Nevada* a Marine band played the "Star-Spangled Banner" while a color guard hoisted the American flag. In the middle of the ceremony the rear gunner of a Japanese aircraft sprayed the ship with machine-gun fire. No one was hit, but bullets ripped into the flag. The highly disciplined Marine Corps band continued to play the national anthem, hardly missing a beat. At the last note, however, everyone scattered for cover.

A wave of Japanese torpedo planes skimmed over the water toward the *Oklahoma.* At close range they dropped their torpedoes, which splashed into the water and arrowed toward the mighty battleship. Three of them crashed into the *Oklahoma's* side. "There was a tremendous explosion," Seaman Fomby remembered. "The ship weighed about 30,000 tons, and when the torpedoes hit they shook everything on her."[2]

The explosions along the line of vessels the sailors called Battleship Row shattered the peaceful Sunday morning. Suddenly excited voices from ships' loudspeakers burst out the electrifying news:

AIR RAID! AIR RAID! THIS IS NO DRILL!

A half dozen bombers, looking like huge dragonflies, swooped down on the U.S.S. *Arizona.* When they reached a height no greater than that of a telephone pole, they released their bombs. At least one bomb crashed through the *Arizona's* deck and exploded deep within her. Men on neighboring ships claimed they saw the 35,000-ton *Arizona* jump up a foot. The great ship erupted into an orange ball of flame. Almost instantly she sank and settled in the mud off Ford Island. Only her upper decks, swept with fire, protruded from the water.

At nearby Hickham Field, the Japanese planes found hundreds of American aircraft parked neatly, wingtip to wingtip. The attacking Japanese flew so low that men on the ground could see their faces. Some of the enemy pilots were grinning. One frustrated mechanic on the field threw a wrench at a low-flying bomber. American flyers frantically ran for their planes, but only one pilot managed to get his craft off the ground during the first wave of the attack. The Japanese bombed and machine-gunned the American planes at will.

An hour after the first attack, a second wave of 160 Japanese fighters and bombers roared in from their carriers. But the second group faced an alerted American force. The sky was now peppered with black clouds of

The U.S.S. *Arizona* spews smoke and fire after being hit repeatedly by Japanese bombs during the surprise attack on Pearl Harbor. More than 1,000 American sailors died on the battleship.

smoke from anti-aircraft artillery. American planes took off to dogfight with the raiders. Still the Japanese inflicted further damage on the already battered ships and aircraft. Pearl Harbor was a hell of fire and thick, billowing smoke.

As night fell, medical personnel treated thousands of wounded. Crews battled fires blazing on the decks of the ships of Battleship Row. Men and women stationed at Pearl Harbor saw first-hand the ghastly face of war. Marine PFC James Cory, a survivor of the holocaust that erupted on the *Arizona*, came across a group of horribly

A burned and crippled B-17 bomber sits on Hickam Field at Pearl Harbor on December 7, 1941. The Americans lost 350 aircraft destroyed or damaged during the raid.

burned sailors: "These people were zombies in essence. They were burned completely white. . . . Their hair was burned off; their eyelashes were burned off. . . . They were moving like robots. . . . Their arms were out, held away from their bodies. . . . These were burned men!"[3]

Later the Americans counted their losses. In the 90-minute battle, 350 aircraft had been destroyed or damaged. Six of the eight battleships docked at Pearl Harbor had been sunk or were in ruins. A dozen other warships had been bombed or torpedoed. All the damage was inflicted by Japanese aircraft; their submarines, which were supposed to launch a separate attack, had failed to score even one hit with their torpedoes. The loss of life at Pearl Harbor was appalling. Some 2,400 military personnel and civilians had been killed. More than 1,000 sailors died on the battleship *Arizona* alone. Their ship became their tomb—the *Arizona* was never raised.

A day after the devastating attack, President Franklin Delano Roosevelt spoke before the American Congress. He called December 7, 1941, "a date which will live in infamy." The president asked for and received permission from Congress to declare war on Japan. Three days later, Germany and Italy—who were allied with Japan—declared war on the United States.

Pearl Harbor catapulted the United States into World War II. This war was a two-ocean conflict that saw Americans serving on opposite sides of the world. And for thousands of American soldiers, sailors, and marines the cruelest battles would be fought in the Pacific.

Franklin D. Roosevelt was president at the time of the Japanese attack on Pearl Harbor and led the country through most of World War II until his death on April 12, 1945.

Every home is a battleground now! We are all comrades in arms! We must fight through to the end. . . . Let us sacrifice every bit of our lives for the Emperor!
—Japanese government radio broadcast early in 1942.

2 The Rising Sun Over The Pacific

In 1937 an ancient stone bridge, named after the explorer Marco Polo, that spanned a river near the Chinese city of Pei-p'ing (now Beijing) became part of history. On the night of July 7 a Japanese army unit maneuvering near the bridge was fired upon by Chinese troops. Japanese army units had been in mainland China since 1931, when Japan began its occupation of the Chinese region of Manchuria. Some historians believe the Japanese takeover of Manchuria was the true beginning of World War II. The few shots at the Marco Polo Bridge were probably fired by accident, but they sparked an undeclared war between China and Japan.

Spearheading the Japanese war machine were modern

bombers that pounded Chinese cities. Aerial warfare was new at the time. Never before had civilians been subjected to such ferocious attacks from ᵗhe sky. Under a rain of bombs, flimsy wooden houses typical of Chinese cities erupted in flames. People trapped in narrow back alleys were roasted to death in firestorms. The twisting streets became a nightmare of cries: Mothers shrieked for lost children, people with ghastly burns screamed in pain, elderly men and women chanted prayers.

A terrified baby, one of the few survivors of a Japanese air raid that leveled the railroad station in Shanghai, China, in August, 1937. This particularly heart-wrenching picture shocked and infuriated Americans.

The Warlords

Aided by the bombers, the ruthlessly efficient Japanese army swept over much of eastern China. The conquest of Chinese territory pleased the Japanese warlords, a small group of powerful military leaders and politicians. The warlords had come to power in the early 1930's when Japan was in the throes of the worldwide economic depression. They convinced the Japanese people that the nation must expand in order to rescue itself

These Chinese civilians were killed outside an air raid shelter in the city of Chungking in June, 1941. Many of the victims were trampled to death as mobs of people, terrified of Japanese bombers, tried to push their way into the shelter's entrance.

from poverty. Japan needed raw materials—iron ore, rubber, and oil—to nourish its industries. According to the warlords only military conquest could bring the nation what it needed to survive.

The 1930's was a decade ripe for the rise of political strongmen who would steer their countries toward war. On the other side of the world, Germany's Adolf Hitler and Italy's Benito Mussolini armed their nations and pursued a foreign policy aimed at the conquest of other lands. Germany and Italy had loose military alliances with Japan, but all three countries went about their courses of conquest independently.

One of the leading Japanese warlords was Hideki Tojo, a general turned politician. Nicknamed "the Razor," he was a hard-driving, ambitious man who believed war would bring riches and glory to Japan. Tojo became Prime Minister just before the attack on Pearl Harbor. The conduct of the war was largely in his hands.

Americans looked on with alarm as Japan overwhelmed China. For decades China and the United States had enjoyed friendly relations. Now Americans were shocked when they saw news photos of civilian air raid casualties in Chinese cities. In a 1937 speech, President Franklin Roosevelt anguished over the situation in China, ". . . civilians including women and children are being ruthlessly murdered with bombs from the air." The president claimed the Japanese air raids were part of "[an] epidemic of world lawlessness."[1] Roosevelt then announced that America would cut off trade to all

Adolf Hitler, the leader of Nazi Germany, was one of several political strongmen who rose to power in the 1930's when economic depression gripped the world.

aggressor nations. The 1937 move to "quarantine the aggressors" was the United States' first serious step against the warrior nations of Europe and Asia. For Japan it meant an embargo on oil, iron ore, and scrap iron—the goods the Japanese coveted.

The embargo convinced Tojo and the other warlords that the United States was intent on stopping Japanese expansion. Diplomats began a series of talks with the United States, but Japanese leaders did not believe the American president would lift the embargo. So the warlords discussed a move that would prove to be fatal for their nation: war between Japan and America.

Arguing against war was a brilliant naval strategist named Isoroku Yamamoto. He had traveled extensively in the United States, and had seen its steel mills and sprawling factories. Yamamoto believed Japan was bound to lose a war against such an industrial giant as the United States. But the warlords overruled the admiral. Reluctantly Yamamoto planned a first strike on the American naval base at Pearl Harbor. He hoped to obliterate much of the American Pacific fleet in one surprise blow. Such a success would give him time to make other conquests in the Pacific. Yamamoto enjoyed playing poker. During poker games his favorite tactic was to break his opponent's nerve by betting heavily on one strong hand. No doubt Yamamoto, the poker player, was pleased when he heard the code words TORA! TORA! TORA! He knew he had won the first hand in the deadly game of world war.

Admiral Isoroku Yamamoto, Japan's greatest naval leader, masterminded the attack on Pearl Harbor. Yamamoto had lived briefly in the United States, and he cautioned the warlords against the American conflict.

Early Japanese Victories

For generations, much of Asia was locked in the grip of colonialism. The French had colonized Indochina. The Dutch owned what is now Indonesia. The British claimed India, Burma, and Malaya—and had a crown colony at Hong Kong. The United States held dominion over the Philippines. The European and American colonists in Asia often lived in grand houses, surrounded by servants. They regarded Asian lands as an extension of their own countries, a part of their realm. The Dutch governor-general of Indonesia once said, "We Dutch have been here [in Asia] for three hundred years, and we shall remain for another three hundred."

But Japanese expansion spelled doom for the confident colonial powers. The surprise attack on Pearl Harbor was planned to coincide with a series of assaults on European and American territory in Asia. Just hours after the first bombs struck Hawaii, enemy planes attacked Singapore and Hong Kong, and Manila in the Philippines. Boldly the Japanese waged war not only on the United States, but also on Asia's western colonies.

The conquest of Malaya, Great Britain's rich colony in Southeast Asia, was a prime goal for the warlords. In early December, 1941, transport ships pushed up to beaches in the northern Malay peninsula and thousands of Japanese troops splashed ashore. Two of Great Britain's finest battleships, the H.M.S. *Repulse* and the H.M.S. *Prince of Wales,* raced north on December 10th to repel the invasion. Because an earlier Japanese raid had destroyed most of the British air squadrons stationed at Malaya, the great ships were forced to sail without the benefit of fighter planes as an escort.

"Aircraft!" shouted a lookout aboard the *Repulse* as it steamed northward. "Airplanes, off the port side!"

Diving out of the clouds like hawks, a group of Japanese bombers and torpedo planes swooped down on the British vessels. Anti-aircraft guns barked out a furious hail of bullets and shells, but the nimble planes evaded the fire. Bombs and aerial torpedoes ripped into the two ships. Both sank in a matter of hours. More than 800 British seamen lost their lives. In London British Prime Minister Winston Churchill was informed of the disaster

Winston Churchill, Great Britain's wartime leader saw many of Britain's prime Far Eastern colonies such as Hong Kong and Malaya fall to the Japanese in the months after Pearl Harbor.

at sea. "I was glad to be alone [when I was told]," he later wrote. "In all the war I never received a more direct shock."[2]

On land the Japanese troops trekked down the Malay Peninsula toward their ultimate goal: the British colony of Singapore. To reach Singapore the Japanese had to march through almost 500 miles of virtually unpassable territory. The Malay Peninsula is covered with thick jungle rising from a bed of mud and deadly quicksand. Years earlier British military engineers had been convinced the jungle was so forbidding that Singapore was safe from land assault. So the only ammunition supplied for the city's guns were armor-piercing shells which were to be used against attacking ships. These shells were useless against attacking land troops.

Despite jungle terrain and British resistance, the Japanese troops advanced ever closer to Singapore. Where roads did not exist, they cut through vines and underbrush with machetes. The soldiers made crude rafts from trees and floated heavy guns, tanks and ammunition down jungle rivers. The army was not overburdened with supplies because the men were content to eat just a few handfuls of rice a day. In two months the Japanese force, composed of 70,000 troops, arrived at the outskirts of Singapore. Their ground artillery and aerial bombers bombarded the city, killing thousands of civilians. British General A. E. Percival was forced to surrender Singapore on February 15, 1942. Some 85,000 British soldiers were taken prisoner. It was the worst defeat in the history of the British army.

The Philippines, Guam, and Wake Islands

Confusion reigned among the American forces in the Philippines when they heard reports that Pearl Harbor had been attacked. Air officers wanted to send their long-range B-17 bombers 600 miles north to strike Japanese airfields on the island of Formosa. Army General Douglas MacArthur, the overall commander of the Philippines, passed the decision to Major General Lewis Brereton, commander of all U.S. Army Air Forces in the Far East. Brereton refused to authorize the bomber raid. While the top-ranking officers argued, nothing was done to protect Clark Field, America's largest air base on the Philippines.

Japanese planes attacked at noon (Philippine time) on December 8. The pilots found American aircraft at Clark Field parked neatly side by side, as if the machines were awaiting inspection. The enemy roared over the airstrip with machine guns blazing. The B-17's, which had full gas tanks in anticipation of a bombing run, exploded into dazzling mushrooms of flame. In less than an hour the invaders destroyed more than 100 aircraft, including an entire squadron of B-17 heavy bombers. For the American Far East air command, the raid at Clark Field was almost a second Pearl Harbor.

Guam and Wake Islands, two American outposts in the Pacific, were bombed within hours of the assault on Clark Field. Japanese troops stormed ashore on Guam after the bombing. The island, which lay 1,500 miles east of Manila, was defended by about 400 Marines whose heaviest weapons were a few World War I machine guns. Guam fell to the Japanese in a matter of days.

At dawn on December 11, a Japanese flotilla approached the beaches at Wake Island, 2,300 miles west of Pearl Harbor. Perhaps the Japanese naval officers expected an easy victory such as their comrades had enjoyed at Guam. But on this island the American defenders were armed with 5-inch shore guns.

"Fire!" ordered Wake Island commander Scott Cunningham.

With a roar of thunder the guns began their deadly work. "It was a sweet, wonderful, glorious shoot-up," Commander Cunningham wrote later. "The guns hit a light cruiser on the second salvo. [The cruiser] turned and began to run. . . . Battery L was red hot. Three ships were in sight; the gunners chose one and let fire. Dead on target! The crews cheered."[3]

The Wake Island gunners achieved a miracle. Their deadly, accurate fire chased the Japanese fleet away from the beaches. It was, in fact, the first American victory over the Japanese navy in World War II. But the enemy returned with an even larger fleet. This time the Japanese landed 2000 elite marines on the shore. Wake Island was captured. Commander Cunningham and the survivors of the battle spent the rest of the war in Japanese prison camps.

The Fall of the Philippines

A far greater crisis loomed in the Philippines. In late

December Japanese troops landed both north and south of Manila. The invading army was spearheaded by light tanks. Defending the roads to Manila were Philippine reserve troops armed only with rifles. The inexperienced and poorly trained reservists fled in panic before the tanks. Manila was trapped in what military strategists call a "pincer movement:" two army columns closing in on an objective like the pincers of a giant crab. The Philippine capital surrendered to the Japanese on January 2, 1942.

The remaining defenders of the Philippines rallied behind their commander, General Douglas MacArthur. MacArthur was born into military life and grew up on army posts. His father was a famous general who had won the Congressional Medal of Honor for his heroism in the American Civil War. Douglas MacArthur graduated from the military academy at West Point in 1903 as the top student in his class, and he later served as a frontline infantry officer in World War I. In 1930 he was promoted to four-star general, the youngest man ever to achieve that rank.

Following the fall of Manila, MacArthur planned to make a final stand on the Bataan Peninsula, a jungle-covered strip of land some 30 miles long and 15 wide. On Bataan the American army discovered what the British already knew: Japanese soldiers were among the world's best jungle fighters. Slipping through the underbrush at night, small bands of enemy troops ranged far behind American lines to attack rear positions. On the Bataan front the Japanese launched furious attacks

General Douglas MacArthur, the commander of the Philippine forces in 1941. His words "I shall return" became a rallying cry for Americans and Filipinos who looked forward to the liberation of the islands.

while shouting their fearsome battle cry, "Banzai! Banzai!" Even thick rows of barbed wire failed to protect American defenders. Front ranks of charging Japanese threw themselves on the barbed wire and allowed their bodies to be used as bridges over which their fellow soldiers ran.

As one banzai attack followed another, the Japanese pushed the Americans steadily backward on Bataan. The Japanese navy controlled the waters off Manila, cutting off all efforts to resupply American forces. Food supplies dwindled to almost nothing. Some units were reduced to eating rats. Finally, on the morning of April 9, 1942, a string of white flags appeared over the battle-scarred jungle. American headquarters ordered the 75,000 defenders of Bataan, 12,000 of them Americans, to surrender.

The Japanese then subjected their prisoners to what was called the great "Bataan Death March." The weary and disease-wracked men were forced to hike a grueling 65 miles over jungle roads to a railroad center. The horrific trek took six days. A young soldier named Dick Bilyeu survived the Death March and later wrote, "The guards drove us hard. Anyone who stumbled was prodded in the back and forced to his feet. If he fell he was run through with a bayonet or a saber. Nobody was allowed to stop and assist those who fell. . . . When a prisoner fell dead or was murdered, he was left where he had fallen. . . . There was hardly a time when I didn't see a body of someone who had either been killed or had died, left where it had fallen on the road."[4] About 7,000

Americans and Filipinos perished during the infamous march.

General MacArthur was not among the Americans who suffered through the Bataan Death March. He had escaped to Australia aboard a small navy PT boat four weeks earlier. The general left his men reluctantly, and only after President Roosevelt ordered him to evacuate. When he stepped ashore at Australia, MacArthur told a reporter, "I have come through, and I shall return." His words—"I shall return"—became an inspiration for thousands of Americans and Filipinos who dreamed of a future day when MacArthur would drive the Japanese from the islands.

Japan at Its Zenith

Former European colonies and independent countries quickly fell to the Japanese juggernaut. Thailand, Burma, the Dutch East Indies, the Solomon and Gilbert Islands, all were engulfed by the new masters of Asia. Most of the conquests were made within four months of the Pearl Harbor attack. Japanese territory grew to include more than one million square miles on the Asian mainland. Japan also presided over an island empire embracing almost the entire western half of the Pacific Ocean. Above these occupied lands rose the Japanese flag with its proud symbol of the rising sun. That flag attested to all the world that Japan was now the dominant power in the Orient. This small nation achieved its fantastic record of conquest through the efforts of its brave soldiers, the tactics of its bold commanders, and a magnificent air force.

The fanatical courage of Japanese fighting men became the stuff of legend in the Pacific War. Shrieking their battle cry, "Banzai! Banzai!" Japanese soldiers charged their enemy as if they had no fear of death. The word *banzai* means "forever" or "ten thousand years." In the heat of battle it conveyed the message, "Imperial Japan will live for ten thousand years." Bravery was instilled in Japan's future soldiers while they were boys. Teachers and government officials drove into their minds the creed that death in battle was a glorious sacrifice and surrender to the enemy an unthinkable disgrace. This code of conduct was called *Bushido*—the way of the warrior. American sailors saw the results of the Bushido code at various times in the Pacific when, for example, Japanese seamen swam *away* from American ships trying to rescue them from shark-infested waters.

Acting as a heavenly sword for the Japanese army and navy was a splendid air force that boasted skilled pilots and marvelous aircraft. Finest of all the Japanese planes was the single-engine Mitsubishi fighter, which Americans called the Zero. This advanced fighter flew at a top speed of 330 miles per hour, fast by 1941 standards. Sleek and compact, the Zero was able to twist and swerve with the grace of a dancer. Early in the war the Americans had no planes that could match the Zero for speed, range, an maneuverability.

Officers devoted to offensive warfare commanded the men of the rising sun. In battle they strove to hit

The Pacific War

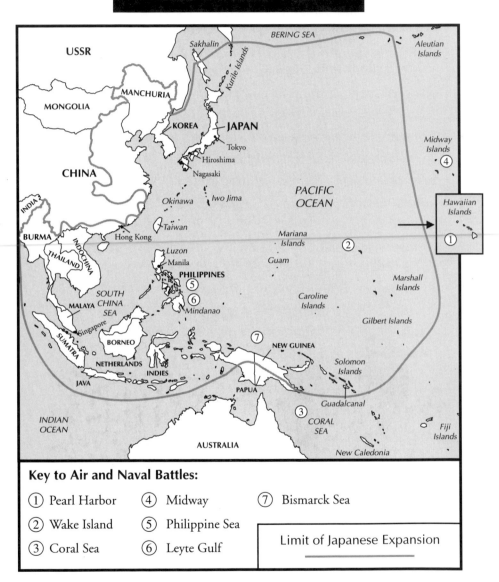

Key to Air and Naval Battles:

1. Pearl Harbor
2. Wake Island
3. Coral Sea
4. Midway
5. Philippine Sea
6. Leyte Gulf
7. Bismarck Sea

Limit of Japanese Expansion

their enemies with unexpected violent blows to shock them into submission. Following Pearl Harbor the offensive-minded Japanese officers became drunk with their own success. Their campaigns over land and sea had carved out the largest empire ever amassed in the Pacific. But while most officers were giddy with such conquests, their commander—Admiral Yamamoto—remained somber. From the beginning Yamamoto had opposed war with the United States because he feared he would waken a sleeping tiger. Worst of all, he dreaded a long war with his potentially powerful enemy. Some weeks before Pearl Harbor, Yamamoto wrote Prime Minister Tojo: "[When war comes] I shall run wild for the first six months or a year, but I have utterly no confidence for the second or third year."

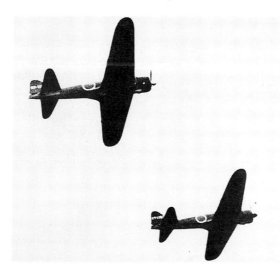

The Japanese Zero fighter plane shocked American flyers. Early in the war the Americans had no plane that measured up to the nimble Japanese fighter.

During the past two weeks we have had a great deal of good news, and it would seem that a turning-point in this war has at last been reached.
—Franklin D. Roosevelt, New York City, Nov. 17, 1942.

3 The Turning of the Tide

On the morning of April 18, 1942, the aircraft carrier U.S.S. *Hornet* steamed over the choppy Pacific. A wind swept the deck with much force that sailors had to lean sharply windward in order to avoid being blown over. On board the flattop were 16 ungainly looking two-engine B-25 bombers. The crews of these planes hoped to launch America's first air raid against Japan.

The Doolittle Raid

With propellers whirling, the lead bomber struggled to move forward against the gale force wind. The plane was piloted by Lt. Col. James H. Doolittle, a World War I aviator. The B-25's were land-based bombers. They were not built to take off from an aircraft carrier whose deck was only slightly longer than two football fields. Ted Lawson, a pilot in the plane behind Doolittle, later wrote, "We watched [Doolittle] like hawks, wondering what the wind would do to him, and whether he could take off in the little run toward the bow. If he couldn't, we couldn't."[1]

With agonizing slowness, Doolittle's aircraft lumbered forward, nosed off the bow, and became airborne. The other planes followed. Miraculously all 16 bombers took off without incident.

The mission, however, was in trouble even before takeoff. Hours earlier the carrier had been spotted by a Japanese patrol ship, forcing Doolittle to start the flight much farther from Japan than he had planned. Originally Doolittle had hoped to fly to friendly airfields in China after the squadron completed its mission. Now it seemed clear that the planes would lack the fuel to bomb their targets in Japan and then reach Chinese territory safely.

A little more than three and a half hours after takeoff, the bombers approached the coast of Japan. The enemy was taken by surprise. Flying along the coast, Doolittle's men encountered no Japanese fighter planes. The bombers struck Tokyo and other targets on Japan's main island. The raid was over in minutes. It did little military damage, but it stunned Japanese political and military leaders, who believed their far-flung island nation was safe from enemy air assault.

Most of the B-25 crews crash-landed or parachuted over Chinese territory. Once on the ground, Chinese

A B-25 struggles to take off from the pitching deck of the American aircraft carrier *Hornet* on April 18, 1942. The large bombers were commanded by Col. James H. Doolittle, who led them on America's first air raid over Japan.

partisans helped the men steal across Japanese-occupied areas and reach friendly lines. Eight flyers, the survivors of two B-25's, were captured by the Japanese. Three of the men were executed after a Japanese court condemned them as "enemies of the people."

Doolittle's raid was a propaganda victory that immediately boosted morale in the United States. Americans, weary of constant defeat, cheered when they heard the news on radio. The *Los Angeles Times* printed a banner headline:

DOOLITTLE DID IT!

The surviving crew members were flown out of China and taken to the White House where President Roosevelt presented the Congressional Medal of Honor, the nation's highest award, to Doolittle. After the ceremony the colonel was interviewed by a reporter from *Life* Magazine. Doolittle told the reporter that at times his plane flew so low he could see the expressions on the faces of Japanese soldiers on the ground.

"And what was their expression?" the reporter asked.

"It was, I should say, one of intense surprise," answered Doolittle.[2]

The Battle of the Coral Sea

In the past, war at sea had meant giant battleships steaming within range of each other and exchanging thundering broadsides. But over the Pacific, a new era in naval warfare now dawned. The Battle of the Coral Sea, fought from May 4 to May 8, 1942, was waged between two fleets that never came within 100 miles of each other.

The history-making battle began when the Japanese attempted to occupy Port Moresby on the southeastern tip of New Guinea. From Port Moresby the Japanese could threaten Australia. Hurrying to counterattack came an American fleet headed by the aircraft carriers *U.S.S. Hornet* and U.S.S. *Lexington.* The air raid at Pearl Harbor had smashed the American battleship arm, but left its carriers untouched. Fortunately for the United States, all four carriers assigned to the Pacific fleet were at sea on "Pearl Harbor Day."

The United States Navy struck first. Flying slow and clumsy Dauntless dive-bombers, American pilots dove at a Japanese carrier. The sky above the carrier buzzed with Zeros, which could fly 50 to 100 miles an hour faster than the American bombers. But the Dauntlesses were ruggedly built and they continued diving even though some were being peppered with Japanese machine-gun bullets. Bombs and torpedoes ripped into the enemy carrier *Shoho.* It burst into flame. One of the American pilots, Lt. Robert E. Dixon, sent a now famous message back to his superior officers: "Dixon to carrier, scratch one flattop."

A wild afternoon and evening followed. Japanese planes searched desperately for the American fleet, but to no avail. After darkness, however, a group of Japanese planes accidentally flew over the U.S.S. *Yorktown;* the pilots thought it was one of their own ships. In the confusion a few Japanese planes actually tried to land on the *Yorktown*'s flight deck.

The next morning Japanese aircraft found and attacked the carrier *Lexington*. Above the ship the sky was filled with American fighter planes trying to defend their ship. The *Lexington*'s gunners hammered out a storm of anti-aircraft fire. A Japanese pilot who flew through this incredible maze later called it, "a fantastic rainfall of anti-aircraft and spinning planes." The *Lexington* was hit with two bombs and two torpedoes. Hundreds of men were killed and wounded on the stricken ship. A dozen fires broke out. The *Lexington*'s commander gave the order to abandon ship. Luckily the carrier sank slowly and 2,735 of her crew were rescued by nearby vessels. The men who were pulled out of the water cried openly when they saw their beloved "Lady Lex" go down.

The Japanese navy had lost a carrier, and so had the American navy. On the surface it appeared that the Battle of the Coral Sea had ended in a draw. But the Japanese were driven away from Port Moresby. The shores of Australia were safe. The stage was now set for another carrier battle that would alter the course of the Pacific War.

Midway—The Turning-Point

In late May, 1942, a radio operator on Midway Island tapped out the message: WE ARE RUNNING LOW ON WATER. The message was a lie—Midway had plenty of water. The lie was manufactured by Joe Rochefort, a naval officer who specialized in deciphering

The aircraft carrier U.S.S. *Lexington* burns furiously after being struck by Japanese bombs and torpedoes during the Battle of the Coral Sea. The much beloved "Lady Lex" later sunk.

enemy codes. Months earlier Rochefort and a team of code-breakers had succeeded in cracking most of the complicated code the Japanese used when sending military messages. They now knew the Japanese planned a major invasion of an island called AF. Rochefort suspected AF was Midway Island. To make certain, he sent out the false statement concerning the water supply. Hours later a Japanese radio operator reported: AF IS RUNNING LOW ON WATER. "Aha," said Rochefort and his code-busters.

Midway Island is a tiny coral atoll that lies about

Carrier-based dive bombers, such as the Dauntless, cruised at altitudes of about 15,000 feet before diving straight down to under 2,000 feet to drop their bombs. Dive bombers destroyed or damaged many Japanese battleships and aircraft carriers.

1,200 miles west of Hawaii. The American navy had occupied this speck on the map for 40 years. The Japanese coveted the island because it could be used as a stepping-stone for an invasion of Hawaii.

Planning the Midway campaign was Admiral Isoroku Yamamoto, the mastermind of the Pearl Harbor raid. The incredible battle began on June 3, 1942, but not at Midway Island. Hundreds of miles to the north, Japanese carriers launched planes and raided American bases on the Aleutian Islands. The Aleutians are the chain of islands that trail away from Alaska. The raid was a diversionary tactic designed by Yamamoto to lure the American fleet temporarily north so Japanese troops could land at Midway without interference from the American navy. It was a sound idea, but the American overall commander, Admiral Chester Nimitz, was not fooled by the Aleutian attack. Thanks to the code-busters, Yamamoto's battle plan was an open book to Nimitz. He ordered American carriers to steam to Midway and prepare for battle.

Admiral Nimitz was the U.S. Navy's most respected strategist. A graduate of the Naval Academy at Annapolis, he was a devoted student of naval operations in previous wars. Under Nimitz' leadership, the Navy rose from a demoralized force following Pearl Harbor to become an aggressive fleet ready and willing to do battle with the pride of the Japanese navy.

Near Midway, planes roared into the sky from the four carriers under Yamamoto's command: the *Akagi, Kaga, Soryu,* and *Hiryu.* American fighters intercepted

Dauntless dive bombers seen carrying out a mission during the Battle of Midway in June, 1942.

the raiders, but they were no match for the classy Zero. The swift and sleek Zeros shot down two-thirds of the American planes. Japanese bombers blasted hangars and oil tanks on the island's air base. Still, the Japanese flight commander thought he had not done enough damage to Midway's air facilities. He radioed his superior officers, requesting another strike.

Meanwhile confusion gripped Japanese commanders on the four carriers. Reports drifted in that an American fleet had been spotted. But the reports were sketchy, and it was not clear if the enemy fleet included aircraft carriers. Because of the confusion, Japanese officers began issuing contradictory orders. At first they told the deck crews to arm planes with torpedoes so they could sink the enemy fleet. Then they changed their orders, commanding the crews to reload the planes with bombs in order to attack Midway Island a second time. The mixed orders left the decks littered with live bombs and highly explosive torpedoes—a potentially disastrous situation.

Flying just a few feet above the waves, 14 American torpedo bombers from the carrier *Hornet* spotted the Japanese ships. Scores of Zeros swarmed upon the American planes, and ten of the fourteen were shot down. Torpedoes dropped by the others sped wide of their marks. The mission failed, but the Zeros had been drawn low to ward off the torpedo planes. Suddenly a second American attack came from above. A group of 37 Dauntless dive bombers screamed down toward the car-

The U.S. aircraft carrier U.S.S. *Yorktown* lists badly after being struck by Japanese bombs and torpedoes during the Battle of Midway. The *Yorktown* sank, but the Japanese lost four carriers—the heart of their fleet—during the battle.

riers. This time the Zeros were unable to climb fast enough to intercept the bombers.

The air was filled with black puffs of smoke from anti-aircraft artillery. Strings of deadly orange tracer bullets arched toward the fast-closing bombers. One bomber pilot, Lt. Wilmer Gallaher, wove through the tracers and took aim at the blood-red rising sun that was painted near the bow of a Japanese carrier. He released his bomb and looked back to follow its flight—something he had been instructed never to do. The bomb tore into the insides of the great ship and a mighty explosion rocked Gallagher's plane.

Bombs from other Dauntlesses drilled into the other carriers as well. Because their decks were cluttered with bombs and torpedoes, the initial explosions caused a terrible series of secondary explosions. Planes parked on the flight deck were left a twisted maze of wreckage. Three of Yamamoto's carriers—the *Akagi, Kaga,* and *Soryu*—were hit and mortally damaged. The pride of the Japanese navy was bled dry in one shocking aerial attack. In just five minutes the course of the Pacific War was altered forever.

When the Dauntlesses flew back to their carrier, a squadron of eighteen Japanese dive bombers followed them at a safe distance. Unwittingly the returning Americans led the enemy right to the carrier *Yorktown.* American fighter planes pounced on the Japanese bombers, but the enemy fought through the fighter screen. Bombs struck the *Yorktown,* knocking out boilers and starting fires.

"Abandon ship! All hands abandon ship!" came a voice on the *Yorktown*'s loudspeaker. The crippled carrier was sunk a day later by a Japanese submarine.

Only one of Yamamoto's carriers, the *Hiryu*, remained untouched. But American bombers spotted the sole survivor amid the smoking wreckage of the Japanese fleet. The Japanese could put up only feeble fighter resistance, because most of their planes had been lost with the damaged and sunken flattops. The Americans scored hits and flames engulfed the *Hiryu*'s deck. It was soon swallowed up by the sea.

The battle ended. The Japanese had lost four of their finest carriers; the Americans had lost the *Yorktown*. In addition, many highly trained Japanese pilots were killed, and some 300 of their top of the line planes were destroyed. All told, 3,500 Japanese perished during the battle. It was the turning point in the war, a disaster from which Tojo and the warlords would never recover. Samuel Eliot Morison, the United States Navy's official historian of World War II, said of the June, 1942, battle, "Midway thrust the warlords back on their heels, caused their ambitious plans . . . to be canceled, and forced on them an unexpected, unwelcome, defensive role."[3]

Guadalcanal

"Now land the landing force," was the order barked out on a dozen troop ships. Bending under the weight of their 40-pound packs, 11,000 marines stepped over troop ship rails and climbed down cargo nets to landing craft. It was August 7, 1942. Ahead of the marines was

Marines landing on the island of Guadalcanal in the Solomon
Islands.

The aircraft carrier USS *Wasp* begins to sink after being struck by torpedoes fired from a Japanese submarine on September 15, 1942.

the jungle-covered island of Guadalcanal in the Solomon Islands. America's first offensive operation in the Pacific had begun.

Landing was easy. The marines splashed ashore without a shot fired at them. One of the first Americans on Guadalcanal's beach was a newspaperman named Richard Tregaskis. He later wrote, "We rested in a coconut grove for a few minutes before moving on. It was quite peaceful . . . for it was now the general assumption amongst our group that there were no Japs in the vicinity."[4] The only American casualty in the Guadalcanal landings was a young marine who cut his hand trying to open a coconut with a bayonet.

At sea, operations did not go so smoothly.

On a pitch-dark night, just 48 hours after the marines waded ashore, a group of American and Australian ships patrolled the waters off Guadalcanal. No one on the Allied ships saw the Japanese cruisers approaching. Japanese sailors were specially trained for night attack. Every Japanese seaman was tested for night vision, and the best of them were made lookouts on combat vessels. The sharp-eyed Japanese lookouts guided their ships to the Allied fleet, which steamed near a tiny outcrop of land called Savo Island.

Suddenly the silent, dark night exploded with gunfire. Muzzle blasts and searchlights pierced the blackness. The American cruiser U.S.S. *Chicago* and the Australian cruiser *Canberra* were hit. Fires broke out on their decks. Sailors covered with burns staggered topside, screaming in agony and terror. Shells and torpedoes struck two other Allied cruisers. The Battle of Savo Island lasted forty furious minutes. It ended with the Japanese fleet slipping into open waters, leaving in its wake four sunken ships and 1,000 American and Australian sailors dead. So many ships had gone down that the sea channel between Savo Island and Guadalcanal became known as "Ironbottom Sound."

Victory at sea gave the Japanese commanders confidence to land more troops on Guadalcanal. The island was vital to both sides because it held a half-completed airfield. Most ground battles took place near this field. On one rainswept night, at a hill called Bloody Ridge, the Japanese used human wave attacks to overthrow marine positions. The Battle of Bloody Ridge was a nightmare. Men flailed at each other with bayonets, rifle butts, and fists. The next morning the marines still held the ridge. The ground in front of them was littered with the mangled bodies of American and Japanese troops.

When not under Japanese attack the marines on Guadalcanal battled the jungle. Tall grasses that covered the island had spines so sharp they could open a man's skin like a knife. Marine foxholes and tents were invaded by hellish visitors—ferocious-looking land crabs, spiders the size of golf balls, and swarming white ants that left vicious bites. So thick were the flies that the marines had to devise a special way of eating: Shake a forkful of food vigorously to dislodge the flies and then snap it into your mouth before they returned. Most of the men still found themselves spitting out a last stubborn fly before swallowing.

The worst of the jungle pests were the mosquitoes, which tormented the men and robbed them of sleep. Many mosquitoes carried the dreaded disease malaria. A man stricken with malaria felt as if he were burning up with fever one minute and shivering with cold chills the next. Malaria and other jungle illnesses caused hundreds of deaths on Guadalcanal.

The struggle for Guadalcanal Island stretched on for six months. Battles raged on sea and on land. Japanese warships steamed close to the island's shores and pounded the marine positions with heavy guns. "It was the noise that got you," a marine sergeant named Kevin McCarthy wrote after suffering through one of these bombardments. "You thought it would never stop. You thought every shell had your number on it."[5]

Small, plywood PT boats attempted to drive the Japanese navy away from Guadalcanal's beaches. One PT was commanded by a young officer from Massachusetts named John F. Kennedy. In a night battle that took place in August, 1942, Kennedy's PT boat was rammed by a Japanese destroyer and cut in two. Despite a painful back injury, Kennedy spent five hours in the water towing a disabled shipmate to shore. For his heroism he was awarded the Navy and Marine Corps Medal. Eighteen years later, John F. Kennedy was elected the 35th president of the United States.

More than 4,000 American soldiers, sailors, and Marines died to secure the treacherous little island of Guadalcanal. Graves dug in the jungle attested to the attrition of the ground troops. Over the grave of one marine was a poem, no doubt written by a buddy, that described the horror of Guadalcanal:

> *And when he goes to heaven*
> *To St. Peter he'll tell:*
> *Another Marine reporting, sir,*
> *I've served my time in hell.*

We must hate with every fiber of our being. We must lust for battle; our object in life must be to kill.
—General Lesley J. McNair, U.S.

We will build a barricade across the Pacific with our bodies.
—General Masaharu Homma, Japan.

The War At Home

Hours after Pearl Harbor the owner of a toy and novelty store in Yonkers, New York, took an axe and chopped up every item in his shop that was labeled "Made in Japan." In a park in Washington, D.C., angry Americans cut down a grove of cherry trees that had been donated to the park years earlier by the Japanese Emperor. In San Francisco groups of young toughs roamed the streets of an Oriental neighborhood looking to beat up a "Dirty Jap."

Americans and the "Dirty Japs"

Dirty Japs—that epitaph was used countless times by Americans during the war years. True, the country was at war with Germany too. But the American people directed their most intense hatred at the Japanese. They were thought of as a savage people not worthy of trust or forgiveness. To millions of white Americans, the Pacific war was a racial war pitting us—the white Christians—against them—the yellow heathens. Hatred flowed easier when funneled toward another race.

Fanning the flames of hatred were the American press, radio, and movies. During the war years newspapers and magazines commonly referred to Japanese people as "Japs" or "Nips." A popular tune on the radio was titled "I'm Gonna Slap a Dirty Little Jap." The movie *Purple Heart*, seen by millions, showed sadistic Japanese officers torturing and finally executing captured American flyers. As one American pilot marches off to his death he shouts at his Japanese captors, "This is your war—you wanted it . . . and you're going to get it and it won't be finished until your dirty little empire is wiped off the face of the earth."[1]

American children too were caught up in the wave of anti-Japanese passion. Parents and older brothers and sisters told young children that the Japanese were bogeymen who would "get you" if they didn't behave. A girl named Sheril Cunning, who lived in La Jolla, California, said, "I remember someone telling [my sister and me] that the Japanese would put bamboo splints under your fingernails and set them on fire."[2]

Hatred of the Japanese reached its cruelest peak on the west coast after the shock of Pearl Harbor. Suddenly stores refused to sell groceries to Japanese shoppers. Gas stations denied them gas. They were even expelled from churches.

Worst of all, Japanese-Americans were suspected of being enemy agents. Rumors circulated that Japanese homes on the west coast were equipped with radios tuned in to Tokyo. People living along the coast claimed they saw their Japanese neighbors on the beaches at night signaling submarines with flashlights. All these rumors and accusations proved to be false. Not one shred of hard evidence came to light that showed that Japanese-Americans were disloyal to their country. But the suspicions, fueled by a mindless hatred, grew like a fire out of control. The government reacted.

In February 1942, President Franklin Roosevelt signed Executive Order 9066. It decreed that all people of Japanese descent—both citizens and aliens—were to be moved from the states of California, Oregon, and Washington. Some 112,000 men, women, and children were forced out of their homes, put on busses and trains, and shipped to barbed-wire-enclosed tent cities far from the Pacific coast. In these "relocation camps" Japanese families lived in dusty barracks that lacked privacy. Never could the inmates forget they were living behind barbed wire and guarded by soldiers carrying rifles. Even President Roosevelt was once heard to call the tent cities "concentration camps," after the notorious Nazi prisons.

Yoshiko Uchida was a young college student when her family was ordered from their San Francisco home. She was shocked and outraged that she—a California-born American teenager—had to be locked up simply because she was of Japanese descent. Years later she wrote about the day her family was forced to relocate.

A Japanese-American family is forced to leave their home near Turlock, California, in May of 1942. People of Japanese ancestry were required to live in barbed wire enclosed compounds away from the west coast.

"We were too tense and exhausted to fully sense the terrible wrench of leaving our home. . . . It wasn't until I saw the armed guards . . . their bayonets mounted and ready, that I realized the full horror of the situation. Then my knees sagged, my stomach began to churn, and I very nearly lost my breakfast."[3]

Despite this brutal treatment, hundreds of Japanese young men volunteered for the American army. Most Japanese soldiers served in the 442nd Regimental Combat Team. Because their loyalty was still suspect the 442nd was not sent to the Pacific front. Still, the Japanese volunteers made the 442nd one of the most famous outfits of the war. In Europe the regiment endured almost two years of constant combat and suffered incredible casualties; yet its men wore more medals for bravery than any other unit its size in the U.S. Army.

America Builds a Fleet

American civilians waged their own war at home, on what journalists called the home front. It was a frenzied war of production—the making of guns, planes, and ships. America's special need in the Pacific was a flotilla of ships to cover that vast sea. During the war, home-front men and women built 11,900 ships, giving the United States a bigger fleet than all the combined navies of the world.

Before the war the American navy had five aircraft carriers, four of them assigned to the Pacific. By 1945 more than 100 new carriers had joined the fleet. Many of the new flattops were "jeep carriers," light vessels designed to carry a small squadron of planes and used mainly to escort convoys. The workhorses of the Pacific fleet were the Essex class carriers. Essex flattops were fast, 35,000-ton ships that carried up to 90 planes. Seventeen of these outstanding carriers were built during the war years. All the Essexes served in the Pacific. They made up a carrier task force the Japanese could not begin to match.

Home-front engineers and designers worked to build the world's best airplanes to serve the new carriers. Ironically they were aided by the outstanding Japanese fighter called the Zero. In early 1942, a Zero crash-landed on an island near Alaska. American soldiers recovered the plane almost intact. Using the captured plane as a model, aircraft designers fashioned a new fighter that could outclimb and outmaneuver the much respected enemy machine. The result was a marvelous plane called the Hellcat, one loved by its pilots. The Hellcat's powerful engine enabled it to skim through the sky at 376 m.p.h., a full 50 m.p.h. faster than the Zero. Home-front factories produced more than 12,000 Hellcats, and they soon mastered the skies over the Pacific.

Of course the navy needed more than just warships. One of the Pacific fleet's primary tasks was transporting war material to far-flung islands. A special class of cargo-carrying vessels called Liberty ships was ideally suited for this job. Liberty ships were graceless looking craft, designed after a British series of tramp steamers. Old-time sailors called the Liberties "ugly ducklings." But they could carry almost 11,000 tons of cargo, and they were

A crewman on an American PT boat aims his dual machine guns. Twin machine guns such as these were designed as antiaircraft weapons.

relatively easy to build. By 1943 home-front shipyards were churning out 140 new Liberties each month.

One-third of the nation's Liberties came from shipyards owned by Henry Kaiser. Before the war Kaiser knew nothing about ship building, yet he revolutionized ship production methods by constructing large sections of Liberty ships on land and then hauling the sections by freight car to the shipyards for final assembly. One of Kaiser's shipyards built a Liberty ship in the record time of ten working days. Even though he was a ship-building genius, Henry Kaiser would never be a true navy man. He continually called the bow of his Liberties the "front end."

The factories and shipyards of the home front changed life for American women. Due to demands for greater production, more than six million women took jobs in American industry. Before the war women were virtually banned from the shipyards because the work there was deemed too heavy for them. But once the shipyard doors were open to them, women took jobs as painters, riveters, and machinists. By 1944 women held ten percent of the nation's shipyard jobs. Without the help of female workers the great American fleet would never have been built.

Coralee Redmond moved her large family, which included six children and several brothers, from a farm in North Dakota to the west coast when the war began. Once there the family had to adjust to the frenzy of the home front. "We went to Tacoma, Washington . . . and we worked in the shipyards," Redmond recalled. "I felt

A woman shipyard worker helps to build a Liberty ship at the Kaiser shipyards of Richmond, California. The woman, Miss Eastine Cowner, worked as a waitress before the war.

my family and I were doing our part with the things that had to be done to help our boys in the service . . . Our one boy who was in grade school picked beans on the local farms. The money he earned, we bought savings bonds for him. . . . Those were busy times."[4]

Sailors for the nation's new fleet came from every part of the country, including landlocked regions where the residents never saw the sea. The five Sullivan brothers from Waterloo, Iowa, knew nothing about seamanship when they joined the Navy shortly after Pearl Harbor. The brothers, who were from a close-knit working class family, insisted they all be stationed onboard the same ship. The Navy agreed, and assigned them to the cruiser U.S.S. *Juneau*. On November 14, 1942, the *Juneau* was sunk in a battle of Guadalcanal. All five Sullivan boys were killed. Not since the Civil War had one American family lost five sons in combat. The Sullivan survivors—mother, father, and sister— were hailed as heroes of the home front.

Life in Japan

Even before the war working-class Japanese lived austere lives. Their diet consisted of little more than rice, noodles, cabbage, and sweet potatoes. Japan, an overcrowded country with marginal farmland, had never been able to feed itself. Historically the Japanese had relied on trade to bring them the food stuffs they could not grow. War crippled this already fragile food supply system. Trade declined because Japan produced more guns and tanks than goods it could exchange for food.

Female factory workers put the finishing touches on bomber nose cones.

And American submarines began strangling the island nation by sinking its commercial ships.

By 1943 rice, Japan's staple food, was in short supply. The government urged Japanese housewives to try making new dishes from rice substitutes. One wartime meal called *nukapan* was a concoction made from rice bran and fried wheat flour. "It smelled like horse dung and made you cry when you ate it," complained one Japanese housewife. Food dominated conversations between neighbors and in families. "My younger brother began to look like one of those starving Indian children: skinny, toothpick legs, and large, distended stomach," said a Japanese schoolgirl named Yasuko Kurachi.[5]

A lively black market in food developed between farmers and city-dwelling factory workers. On Sundays, the only day off for factory workers, entire families would trek out to the farms to see what food was available. Money was almost useless in the black market because farmers preferred to trade goods for food. Consequently a city family was forced "to eat" the bicycle it owned before the war, "eat" the blankets it used in the winter, and "eat" the father's old overcoat. The black market was illegal, but officials tolerated it because the illicit trade kept many city families alive.

Clothing and other everyday items also disappeared from Japanese markets. Cotton grew scarce. Wartime Japanese underwear was made out of a combination of cotton and very rough and scratchy wood pulp. The army grabbed up the nation's leather supply to make boots. Instead of shoes civilians were required to wear clumsy wooden clogs that often fell off after a few steps. The government said wearing the clogs would help the war effort, and called them "patriotic footwear."

Japanese leaders expected workers to produce even though they were poorly clothed and reported to factories with their bellies rumbling from hunger. At the same time the government persisted in taking men out of the work force and putting them in the armed forces. By 1943 more than three million Japanese men were serving in the military. Many of these were skilled workers who years earlier had kept the production lines moving. The supervisor of one electrical factory complained, "We lost 1,000 skilled workers and it took 4,000 unskilled workers to replace them."

Children attended school during the war years, but government propaganda replaced reading and writing. Americans, the teachers warned, were cruel barbarians who would torture and kill Japanese children. Above all, the children were instructed that Japan was a nation superior to all others and that the emperor was a living god. Yasuko Kurachi said, "There was a tiny door on the stage behind the principal. He opened this door of beautiful burnished wood. There was another door behind it. He didn't open that one. Behind that second door was supposed to be the emperor's picture. We never got to see it. It was too holy, too divine, to be looked at."[6]

Sports and recreation were encouraged because it was hoped they would lift the morale of hungry workers. Sumo wrestling matches were well attended throughout the war years. Baseball, the import from the United

States, remained a wildly popular sport, but the government insisted that some of the terms be changed because they were too American. Thus hit and run, which the Japanese pronounced as *hitto endo ran* was "Japanesed" to the word *Kyosada.*

However sports and games could not mask the grimness of life in wartime Japan. The country was drained by the demands of the military. Stark feelings of emptiness and exhaustion overcame the nation. A French journalist stationed in Tokyo wrote, "Tokyo, never a pretty town, has now become an ugly town. The capital wakes up a little dirtier each morning, as though tainted by the sinister night in which it has bathed."

And worse suffering was in store for Japanese civilians. Beginning in late 1944 a deadly storm of bombs poured down from the sky. The raids became a horror the people could not have imagined even in their wildest nightmares.

Life in the Japanese Empire

"Asia for the Asians," proclaimed the victorious Japanese when they took over Burma, Indonesia, the Philippines, Indochina, and other regions that were once colonies of the West. Initially many Asian patriots cheered the Japanese as liberators who would finally drive the white colonists out of the Orient.

But the Asian people quickly discovered that the Japanese were far crueler masters than the Europeans and Americans had been. In one occupied country after another arrogant Japanese officers allowed their men to roughshod over the civilian population. The horrible crime of rape was committed practically everywhere the Japanese army travelled. In Hong Kong alone, hundreds of young girls, including some nuns, were raped and murdered by Japanese soldiers. In other areas occupying Japanese troops demanded to be treated as if they were kings. Laws were passed requiring villagers to bow when they met a Japanese soldier on the street. Filipino citizens were forced to wear rising-sun armbands to demonstrate their loyalty to the emperor.

Bushido, the warrior code of bravery, was a prime reason behind the brutal treatment of captive peoples. Army officers believed that no Japanese man or woman would accept living under a foreign overlord. A proper Japanese would commit suicide rather than submit to any authority other than the emperor. Consequently, the Japanese officers reasoned, a people who would surrender to an enemy army had to be subhumans, men and women without pride.

During the first five months of 1942 some 150,000 American, European, and Australian prisoners of war were taken by the Japanese. Japanese soldiers, who themselves genuinely preferred death to defeat, looked upon these men as cowards. In violation of international agreements, the Japanese used the prisoners as slave laborers in projects designed to strengthen the Empire. Thousands of British soldiers were put to work building a 260-mile-long railroad through the jungles connecting Burma to Thailand. The men toiled under a blistering sun and were fed near starvation rations. So many British soldiers succumbed to jungle diseases that the train line was called "death railroad."

More than a half million European colonists, including women and children, also fell into Japanese hands in 1942. They were herded into prison camps and spent the next four years slowly starving and suffering from abysmal medical care.

Young Asian men and women living in the Japanese empire were routinely rounded up to serve as unpaid workers in factories, mines, and on plantations. One man, a Korean named Choi Chun Su, was forced to join a labor gang in a copper mine. He tried to escape but was captured near the prison camp. Then: "I was tied up with a rope and beaten. I fainted but was revived with a bucket of water. This happened three times. They [the Japanese guards] then placed two iron rods in the stove, heated them up, and burned my back with them. When the heated rod was applied to my back the first time, I smelled burning flesh, but after that I felt nothing because I passed out. . . . Three days later [the supervisor] ordered me back into the mines. Yellow fluid oozed out of the blisters on my back."[7]

"Asia for the Asians" was a hollow cry. The Japanese were hated in every occupied land where the Rising Sun waved. Asians looked upon the Americans as liberators who would some day smash the Japanese Empire.

*We knew we were losing the war. First we lost
Guadalcanal and then we lost Saipan. The
government was saying we weren't losing the
islands, we were just retreating strategically . . . .
They were hiding the bad news.*

—Akira Miuri, Tokyo resident

5 The Pacific Offensive

In late December, 1941, while cruising near
the Philippines, Captain Frederick Warder
in the submarine U.S.S. *Sea Wolf* spotted a huge Japanese seaplane tender resting at anchor. It was a target so
inviting he could scarcely believe the image in his periscope. Warder nosed the *Sea Wolf* to within 4,000 yards
of the ship. At this range, against the motionless ship,
he could not miss. Warder fired four torpedoes and
waited to hear an explosion. Silence. He reversed the
Sea Wolf and fired four more "fish" from his rear
tubes. Again there was no explosion. A frustrated
Frederick Warder headed out to the open sea, shaking

his head in mystification. How could all eight torpedoes have missed such a fat target?

The War Under the Pacific

The answer lay in defective torpedoes. The *Sea Wolf* and other American submarines used the Mark 14 torpedo, developed during the 1930's. It was a sophisticated torpedo with a firing device designed to explode directly under a vessel where its armor was weakest. But engineers never adequately tested the Mark 14. The torpedoes cost $10,000 each, an extremely expensive price tag in the 1930's. To waste such costly "fish" in tests seemed to be an extravagance.

In early 1942 a new commander, Rear Admiral Charles Lockwood, took charge of the U.S. submarine fleet in the Pacific. Lookwood conducted his own tests by firing Mark 14 torpedoes into a huge fishnet. He observed that the torpedo often failed to explode, it ran too deep, and it sometimes blew up far before the target. Working with engineers, Lockwood corrected the many flaws in the Mark 14. However, almost two years dragged by before American subs went to sea with dependable torpedoes. Lockwood and his sub fleet then had to make up for an enormous amount of lost time.

Borrowing German U-boat tactics, Lockwood organized his submarines into "wolf packs" of four to five vessels. The packs waited for their prey in the well-traveled sea-lanes of the Japanese empire. Whenever possible, the subs were directed to enemy ships by reconnaissance aircraft. In January of 1944, submarines sank 300,000 tons of Japanese merchant shipping, the highest monthly total of the Pacific war. The underwater onslaught frustrated the plans of the warlords. Their empire now contained the materials they so desperately needed—rubber and oil from Indonesia, rice from Indochina—but these vital goods could reach Japan only by running a deadly gauntlet of American submarines.

The Japanese navy's total dedication to offensive warfare handicapped it in dealing with the submarine menace. In other navies, fast and nimble destroyers were the primary sub fighters. But Japanese admirals viewed destroyers as daring torpedo boats whose main role was to attack large warships. Destroyer crews lacked training for the less exciting task of protecting slow merchant vessels from submarines.

By war's end, U.S. submarines had sunk 1,113 merchant ships and 201 warships. The fleet's grandest victory came on November 29, 1944, when the submarine U.S.S. *Archerfish* sank the giant Japanese aircraft carrier *Shinano*. The *Shinano*, which was on its very first voyage, was the largest ship sunk by a submarine in the history of naval warfare.

The submarine fleet, however, paid a heavy price for its success. When trapped underwater by an enemy ship the submariners endured the nerve-shattering agony of a depth-charge attack. A seaman named Houston E. Lowder served as a radio and sound equipment operator on the U.S.S. *Batfish* and described being in a submarine under attack while deep beneath the sea: "An explosion shook the *Batfish* from stem to stern . . . the boat

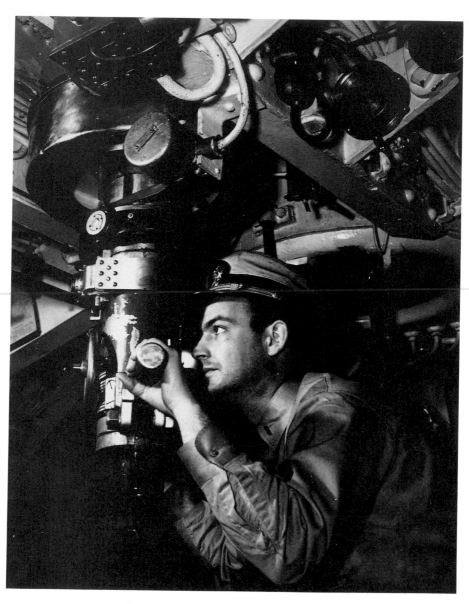

A naval officer peers through the periscope of his submarine.

whipped around like a willow wand. Glass flew from the gauges, cork exploded from the bulkheads like popcorn, light bulbs shattered. Fans and lights went out. . . . Suddenly we were in thick pitch-blackness."[1] During the course of the war 52 American subs were sunk, and 3,505 submariners lost their lives.

Island Hopping

Tiny islands scattered about the Pacific were scenes of some of the most savage fighting of World War II. The Japanese, courageous fighters under any circumstances, battled with the ferocity of cornered animals on island outposts with the ocean at their backs. The Americans in turn bled and died for dots of land they had never heard of before—Guadalcanal in the Solomon Islands, Tarawa in the Gilberts, Saipan and Tinian in the Marianas, Kwajalein and Eniwetok in the Marshalls.

Vice Admiral William "Bull" Halsey was a leading strategist in planning the island campaign. Halsey had certain strongly defended islands bypassed, or "leap-frogged over." Then they were blockaded by American ships and their defenders were left to starve. Halsey ordered the island of Kolombangara in the Solomons bypassed, a decision that probably saved the lives of hundreds of ground troops. In sea combat Halsey was known as a risk taker, a bold commander who was always willing to take a gamble. General MacArthur once called Halsey the war's "greatest fighting admiral."

Marines, who were specially trained for amphibious operations, bore the brunt of the island fighting. Assaulting

This photo of a battered beachhead was taken shortly after the savage Battle of Tarawa ended in November, 1943.

fortified islands followed a grim pattern. First the island was bombed by aircraft. Next the navy moved in battleships and cruisers to pound the beaches with their heavy guns. Then came the command, "Now land the landing force," and the marines crowded into tiny assault boats. The ordeal of island fighting then commenced.

In November 1943, the Marines invaded Tarawa, a coral atoll in the Gilbert Islands. This virtually unknown speck of land in the Pacific came to symbolize the deadly nature of island warfare. Tarawa's central island was only 291 acres in area. Many marines who were farmers in civilian life owned pastures larger than the area over which they were about to risk their lives. Three battleships and dozens of cruisers and destroyers blasted the beaches for hours. Someone with a mind for figures calculated that the navy sent ten tons of high explosive shells into Tarawa for every acre of its land. From the sea the little coral atoll appeared to be awash in hellfire and smoke.

"Now land the landing force."

From the beginning, everything went wrong for the marines at Tarawa. The awesome display of naval firepower seemed to have no effect on the island's defenders. The Japanese gun positions were well dug in and fortified with palm logs and sandbags. Marines were pinned down on the beach by a withering crossfire from dozens of machine guns. Japanese marines, the Emperor's finest troops, defended Tarawa. Their commanding officer boasted, "A million men cannot take Tarawa in a hundred years."

Marines hit the beach at Tarawa, and begin one of the bloodiest battles in the entire "island hopping" campaign.

A second and then a third wave of marines was sent to the beaches. But the tides had shifted, and the landing boats were unable to cross the belt of coral that ringed the island. The marines in later waves had to climb off their boats and wade through the lagoon into the teeth of murderous machine-gun fire. A sailor watching through binoculars said, "Those poor guys plodding in chest-high water and getting shot down. I tried not to look, but I couldn't turn away. The horror of it hypnotized me. If I get to be a hundred years old, I'll always remember."

On the beach a few men rose to become heroes. A Japanese infantry squad crept close to an open-topped landing vehicle and one of them lobbed a hand grenade inside. Marine Corporal John Spillane, a baseball player in civilian life, picked up the grenade and threw it back. The Japanese squad members hurled another grenade, and another. Men watched in horrified fascination as Spillane snatched the grenades out of the air and pitched them into the Japanese position. The deadly game of catch ended when a grenade blew up in Spillane's hand. The shattered hand had to be amputated, and Spillane never played professional baseball as he dreamed he would some day.

Unable to advance, the marines spent their first night on Tarawa huddling on the beaches. The tide moved in, soaking the men. The dead floated eerily among the living. Wounded men moaned. All the marines expected a banzai attack during the night. But the counterattack never came. Naval gunfire had knocked out Japanese telephone lines. Without communications, the enemy could not organize an offensive. The next day the marines slowly, cautiously moved off the beaches. They advanced, but with terrible bloodletting for every yard of ground they gained.

The battle for Tarawa lasted 76 hours; 1,027 Americans were killed, and twice that number wounded. The Japanese fought to the death. Of the 4,700 Japanese defenders, only 17 were taken prisoner. *Time* Magazine correspondent Robert Sherrod reported on the grisly cleanup after the battle: "On the morning of the third day at Tarawa we began burying our dead. It was more gruesome than I can describe. This was no dignified burial—a man's last ceremony should be dignified, but this wasn't. The bulldozer . . . scooped a hole three feet deep. The marines, not even covered by a blanket, were placed in the hole. The bulldozer pushed some more dirt over them, and that was all there was to it."[2]

Tarawa, the island-hopping campaign, and operations in Burma and China allowed Americans and their allies to push ever closer to Japan. On January 31, 1944, American troops attacked the island of Kwajalein in the Marshalls, and on June 15, 1944, the marines invaded Saipan in the Marianas. Each island was a stepping-stone closer to victory in the Pacific war. But looming ahead of the final assault on Japan was the reconquest of the Philippines, the personal goal of General Douglas MacArthur.

Navy pilots loved the F6F Hellcat, but this Hellcat had to crash land on its carrier deck.

The Battle of Leyte Gulf

It was the biggest fleet the sailors had ever seen. Some crewmen tried to count the numbers of ships in the flotilla, but the task was impossible. The ships seemed to spread into infinity, like stars on a clear night. It was October 20, 1944, and landings on the Philippine island of Leyte were about to begin. The landings and the presence of the huge fleet triggered the Battle of Leyte Gulf, the biggest sea battle in history.

The Japanese entered this conflict with a severely weakened air arm. Four months earlier American planes had fought a dramatic duel with Japanese aircraft above the Mariana Islands. The Americans were now armed with the superb Hellcat and a rugged fighter bomber called the Corsair. The Japanese countered with the Zero, certainly a dependable plane, but one that had not been improved since Pearl Harbor. Also, the best of the Japanese pilots had been killed at Midway or in other encounters. The result was a slaughter in the skies. The Japanese lost almost 500 planes. American pilots were amazed by the ease of their victory. One pilot, who was from the South, drawled, "Heck, this was just like a turkey shoot." The air battle was thereafter unofficially called the Great Marianas Turkey Shoot.

Desperate to stop the Philippine assault at Leyte, the Japanese threw the remainder of their navy into action. The brilliant admiral Isoroku Yamamoto had been killed earlier when American fighters shot down a transport plane in which he was a passenger. The Japanese navy

A Japanese torpedo bomber explodes after being hit by antiaircraft fire from an American aircraft carrier.

missed his leadership in the crucial series of battles near Leyte.

The opening blows fell on the Japanese. Submarines spotted the main fleet led by Admiral Takeo Kurita and sank two cruisers and disabled a third. The next morning American bombers sank the battleship *Musashi*, Kurita's second largest vessel. But the Japanese scored a tactical victory when Admiral Halsey, always an aggressive leader, sailed north to pursue a second Japanese fleet composed of three carriers. This was precisely what the Japanese admirals hoped Halsey would do. The ships to the north were a decoy, designed to draw American vessels away from the landing beaches at Leyte. Halsey had swallowed the Japanese bait.

On the morning of October 25, Admiral Kurita led four battleships, six cruisers, and numerous destroyers through the San Bernardino Strait and into the heart of the landing areas at Leyte. To his delight Kurita discovered a group of American escort carriers protected only by destroyers. This situation—battleships versus carriers—was a battleship commander's dream come true. The American carriers launched planes, but in their haste to get off the deck most of the aircraft were unable to load bombs. A few American planes lacked even bullets for their machine guns. Still they buzzed the battleships, hoping to slow down the enemy fleet. Admiral Kurita ordered his battleships to open fire. Quickly Kurita sank one American carrier and three destroyers. One sailor said the heavy Japanese shells pounding into a pounding into a thin-skinned destroyer, "looked like a truck crushing a puppy."

Then suddenly, inexplicably, Kurita ceased fire and pulled his ships away from the melee. American commanders were both shocked and relieved that the Japanese admiral stopped short of annihilating the carrier fleet. Historians now believe Kurita feared a massive American air strike and wanted to protect his ships. Certainly his actions were uncharacteristic for a Japanese naval officer trained to attack aggressively without concern for possible losses.

Meanwhile Admiral Halsey's ships far to the north smashed the Japanese fleet that was serving as a decoy. A total of four separate battles took place in the waters near Leyte Gulf from October 23 to October 26. Books have been written re-creating the details of those bloody episodes. The end result of the series of battles was an overwhelming American victory. The Japanese lost three battleships, four carriers, and ten cruisers. The once proud imperial navy was in shambles.

But an ominous event took place during the height of battle, when a lone Japanese airplane dove at the American escort carrier U.S.S. *Santee*. Ships sent up a wall of anti-aircraft fire, but the pilot continued his determined, almost mad dive. With a terrible explosion, the plane crashed on the carrier's deck. It marked the American navy's first encounter with a kamikaze aircraft. The kamikazes were planes loaded with bombs flown by a pilot bent on killing himself but taking an enemy ship with him in death. In future sea battles, the kamikazes terrorized the American fleet.

MacArthur Returns

"This is the voice of freedom, General MacArthur speaking. People of the Philippines: I have returned!" With these words, General Douglas MacArthur began a speech over Philippine radio just moments after he waded ashore on Leyte Island. He had indeed returned, fulfilling the pledge he made after his escape from Bataan almost three years earlier.

The landings at Leyte met only sporadic Japanese resistance. In many areas, the Americans were overcome by Filipino well-wishers. Robert Shaplen, a writer for the *New Yorker* magazine, said, "In a half hour there were a hundred [Filipinos] milling around us. . . . The young men were exuberant. They wanted, even more than food—which they obviously needed badly—guns so they could join in the fight against the Japs."[3]

Japanese ground forces were commanded by Lieutenant General Tomoyuki Yamashita, who planned to fight a bitter defensive action. But just one glance at a map shows the Philippines to be a complex of large and small islands that can only be supplied by sea. With Americans in control of the air and the sea, Yamashita was unable to bring his troops food and ammunition. A letter, written by a Japanese infantryman and found by an American soldier on Leyte, illustrated the Japanese plight: "I am exhausted. We have no food. The enemy are now within 500 meters of us. Mother, my dear wife

General Douglas MacArthur wades up to the beach at Leyte in the Philippines on October 20, 1944, fulfilling his pledge "I shall return."

and son, I am writing this letter to you by dim candle-light. Our end is near."

In January, 1945, American soldiers landed on Luzon, the main island of the Philippines. With the aid of a parachute jump force and a second amphibious landing by marines, American forces surrounded Manila. There Japanese resistance stiffened. Every building in the capital's outskirts became a lair for machine guns or snipers. MacArthur ordered heavy artillery to pound the city. "Day and night the shelling goes on," wrote a reporter. "How many hundreds or thousands of civilians have already died [in Manila] nobody knows."

Manila fell to the Americans in early March, 1945. More than 100,000 men, women, and children perished in the Philippine capital. They died under the artillery bombardment and at the hands of Japanese troops who ran amok, raping, looting, and killing. The city of Manila, once so lovely it was called the Pearl of the Orient, was reduced to ruins. Hundreds of fires burned out of control. Corpses, rotting under the tropical sun, littered the streets. General MacArthur canceled the victory parade he had intended to stage in the capital. There was no victory to celebrate. Manila was a victim, not a prize of war.

May we walk on the ashes of Tokyo.
—General Simon Bolivar Buckner, Jr., killed on Okinawa,
    the highest-ranking American officer to die in the
    Pacific War.

6 Victory In The Pacific

The moan of air raid sirens broke the night stillness over Yawata, a grimy steel mill town in southern Japan. From a distance came the rumble of powerful aircraft engines. Searchlights flicked on, sending long fingers of light into the blackened skies. A Japanese observer on the ground at Yawata wrote, "I could see clearly the figures of the enemy planes. At once anti-aircraft began to shoot. . . . But the hateful enemy planes flew on. Then came big black things from the white bodies of the planes . . . boom! boom! boom! The devils. The beasts!"

Bombers Over Japan

It was June 15, 1944. The bombing at Yawata was no

ordinary raid. It marked the first time that the B-29 Superfortress, a giant four-engine bomber, was used against Japan. The biggest combat plane of World War II, the B-29's wing span was almost half the length of the football field. The new plane was able to carry 20,000 pounds of bombs, fly at a speed of 357 m.p.h. and had a range of 3,800 miles. Veteran airmen saw the B-29 as a revolutionary machine, one they hoped would blast Japan's industries into nothingness and force that nation's leaders to stop the war.

In early 1945, the huge new planes began taking off from airfields built on the newly captured islands of Saipan, Tinian, and Guam in the Marianas. The bomber chief was a no-nonsense general named Curtis E. LeMay. General LeMay was disappointed with the results of the early B-29 raids that had struck industrial concentrations. He proposed area bombing—sending the B-29's, loaded with incendiary bombs, over cities at night. Incendiaries were small bombs designed to hit the roofs of buildings and burst into flames. Area bombing with incendiaries had a logic that was both simple and terrible: If a whole city is consumed by fire, then its factories and other buildings of military worth would certainly burn with it.

The first massive fire bomb raid took place over Tokyo on the night of March 10, 1945. The largest B-29 force ever assembled—325 bombers—took off from the Marianas and hours later was over Tokyo. "With eight tons of incendiaries crammed into the bomb bay of every Superfort, it didn't take long before there were small

The B-29 was the biggest operational combat plane ever built. It carried ten tons of bombs.

tongues of fire throughout the Tokyo urban area," wrote General LeMay. "Quickly these small fires spread and merged into larger fires, which in turn merged into a firestorm of incredible proportions. The firestorm consumed so much oxygen that those who did not die by the flames simply suffocated . . . it was as through Tokyo had dropped through the floor of the world and into the mouth of hell."[1]

One of the survivors of LeMay's raid was Robert Guillain, a French newsman who lived in Tokyo with his Japanese wife. Guillain wrote: "Bombs were raining down by the thousands . . . setting fire to everything and spreading a wash of dancing flames. . . . Roofs collapsed under the bombs' impact and within minutes the frail houses of wood and paper were aflame. . . . Wherever there was a canal, people hurled themselves into the water; in shallow places people waited, half sunk in noxious muck, mouths just above the surface of the water. Hundreds of them were later found dead; not drowned, but asphyxiated by the burning air and smoke. In other places the water got so hot that the luckless bathers were simply boiled alive."[2]

When the flames finally burned themselves out, the dazed citizens of Tokyo counted their losses. Some 83,000 men, women, and children were dead. More than a quarter million buildings were destroyed. At least half the city was homeless. General LeMay called the air raid an overwhelming success, never mentioning the human suffering on the ground.

More and more giant B-29's rolled off assembly lines

on the home front. Air bases on the Marianas trembled as the giant bombers landed and took off in thunderous relays. Before the end of the war 66 Japanese cities were fire-bombed. Under the shadows of the B-29's the Rising Sun nation was reduced to ashes.

Iwo Jima

No one would argue that Iwo Jima was an ugly little island. It was a rock of a place, eight miles square, made up of volcanic ash and devoid of water or trees. The island's location is what made it important. It lay in the middle of the flight path between the B-29 bases on the Marianas and the major targets in Japan. In American hands fighter planes could take off from Iwo Jima and accompany the big bombers on their raids. Also, damaged B-29's could use Iwo Jima as an emergency landing field. "Without Iwo Jima I can't bomb Japan effectively." General Curtis LeMay told the navy,

D-day dawned, February 19, 1945. Once more marines raced out of landing craft to assault an island they had never heard of. Once more they were greeted by a deadly chorus of artillery. A newspaper writer named John Lardner ran terrified from the shellbursts, but his feet sank into the soft sand, making him feel as if he were running underwater. "When you stopped running or slogging, you became conscious of the whine and bang of artillery shells dropping and bursting near you. All up and down [our beach] men were lying listening to shells and digging or pressing their bodies closer into the sand around them."[3]

Aerial view of the first wave of landing craft approaching the beach at Iwo Jima on February 19, 1945.

Japan–Iwo Jima–Okinawa

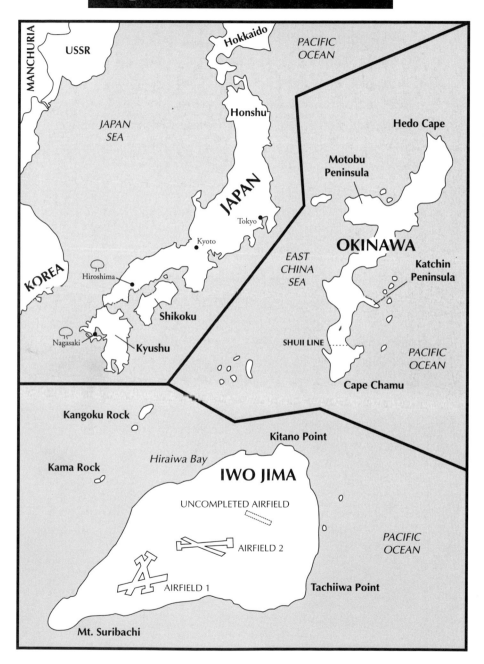

On Iwo Jima the Japanese lay waiting in tunnels, caves, and deep bomb shelters. Their artillery pieces were carefully emplaced in rock and concrete on Mt. Suribachi, the island's only mountain. The 20,000-man force defending Iwo Jima was, according to the Bushido code, prepared to fight until death. Their commander had issued a written order: "Each man will make it his duty to kill ten of the enemy before dying."

Doggedly the marines moved forward. Mostly they advanced on their bellies, slithering through the sand like snakes. All strained to look up at the 500-foot Mount Suribachi, which dominates the island. The marines knew the cone-shaped mountain must be taken. They cursed it.

After three days of ghastly fighting with flamethrowers, bayonets, and grenades a patrol reached the top of

Marines huddle on the beach at Iwo Jima on D-day, February 19, 1945.

Mt. Suribachi. Someone found a long pipe and used it to raise an American flag at the peak. Moments later an enraged Japanese officer rushed out of a cave, shouted angrily at the marines, and tried to cut the flag down with his sword. The Japanese officer was killed by a burst of rifle fire. Next a marine officer trudged up Suribachi and determined the flag was too small. He ordered a larger flag to be raised so that the ships at sea could see the banner. During the second flag-raising photographer Joe Rosenthal snapped a picture. He thought it was a pretty good shot and sent the film back to his ship where the image was transmitted by radio to the United States.

Flag raising on Mount Suribachi, Iwo Jima, February 23, 1945. This dramatic photo was taken by Joe Rosenthal of the Associated Press.

The fighting on the bleak island raged on for a month. In the first few days grisly looking piles of marine bodies grew on the beaches. The dead were coming too fast to be buried. Some 6,000 Marines died on Iwo Jima and 25,000 were wounded. Of the 20,000 Japanese defenders only 216 were taken alive.

At home Americans were shocked by the carnage at Iwo Jima. Key members of Congress questioned the wisdom of attacking such a well-fortified island. But the home front cheered Joe Rosenthal's stunning photo of Mt. Suribachi. The picture of the men raising the flagpole appeared on front pages in newspapers everywhere and came to symbolize the courage of Americans fighting the Pacific War. Admiral Chester Nimitz wrote what amounted to a caption for the picture when he said, "Among the Americans who served on Iwo Island, uncommon valor was a common virtue."

Okinawa

Another island, another hellhole, thought the soldiers and marines who stormed the beaches of Okinawa on April 1, 1945. But Okinawa was only 450 miles from mainland Japan. Many of the people living on the island were Japanese nationals. The Japanese army defending this island would fight with cunning and fury, as if they were protecting the sacred soil of Japan itself.

The landings were easy. Too easy, thought the combat-wise marines and soldiers. Five hours after splashing ashore the Americans captured a key airfield without firing a shot. But a force of 100,000 defenders waited for the Americans at the southern end of the island. Okinawa is both mountainous and jungle-covered—perfect terrain for a defensive war.

To the south, near an ancient castle called Shuri, a hideous battle line developed. As the days and weeks passed the Shuri line became pockmarked and artillery scarred; it bore an amazing resemblance to the battlefields of World War I. A young marine squad leader named William Manchester, who later became a famous author, said of the Shuri line, "It was a monstrous sight, a moonscape. . . . There was nothing green left; artillery had denuded and scarred every inch of ground."[4]

Manchester lost his youthful innocence on Okinawa. He had joined the Marine Corps with dreams of becoming a hero and winning a chest full of medals for bravery. But one by one, on island after island, he saw friends get killed or horribly wounded. The slaughterhouse of Okinawa was the final insult to his illusions: "[On Okinawa] I now knew that banners and swords, ruffles and flourishes, bugles and drums, the whole rigmarole, eventually ended in squalor. . . . My dream of war had been colorful . . . so wholly unrealistic that it deserved to be demolished."[5]

Fierce combat on Okinawa continued for almost three months. Most of the fighting was concentrated in the south where the majority of the island's 400,000 civilians lived. For civilians as well as military men the killing was so terrible it seemed almost unreal. Blood soaked the ground on hills the Americans called Sugarloaf, Half Moon, and Horseshoe. More than 12,500 soldiers, sailors, and marines were killed, and some 30,000 were wounded.

The Divine Wind

While the soldiers and marines struggled to take toeholds of ground a desperate battle took place in the sea off Okinawa. A fleet of 1,500 Allied ships—the largest ever assembled in the Pacific—supported the invasion. Okinawa was well within the range of aircraft taking off from Japan. It was a perfect place for the Japanese to employ suicide pilots, the kamikazes, the last-ditch weapon of the warlords.

The Kamikazes
Like cherry blossoms
In the spring
Let us fall
Clean and Radiant.

This poem was written by a kamikaze pilot shortly before his one-way mission to Okinawa. The last thoughts and writings of the kamikazes were not those of mindless fanatics or drug-crazed madmen, as many Americans considered these pilots to be. Instead they wrote like rational men who deemed it their sad duty to die in war. Before takeoff one of them said to his comrades, "Every man is doomed to go his own way in time." Another wrote, "Think kindly of me and consider it my good fortune to do something praiseworthy."

The word *kamikaze* means "divine wind." It stems from a typhoon that destroyed a Mongol invasion fleet

heading for Japan in the year 1281. The young kamikazes of 1945 thought of themselves as a new divine wind
that would repel American invaders from the shores of
their motherland.

Twenty-one-year-old Ryuji Nagatsuka was a kamikaze. He had been a pilot in training when a call came
for volunteers to join a special suicide squad. Certainly
not every pilot signed up, but the air force had little
trouble filling the kamikaze ranks. Nagatsuka enlisted in
the kamikaze corps because he had a fatal vision he
would die in the war, and he wanted his death to have
purpose.

The night before his mission Nagatsuka carefully cut
his fingernails and a lock of his hair and put them in an
envelope along with a note to his mother and father:
"My dear parents, I shall depart from this life at 0700
hours on the twenty-ninth of June, 1945. My whole being is permeated by your tremendous affection . . . and it
is this which is hard to accept. . . . But patriotic duty demands [my sacrifice]."[6]

Then, moments before he boarded his plane fear and
confusion seized Nagatsuka. He had a passion for French
literature, and now he felt deep regret that he would
have to die without ever again reading a novel he loved.
Did the love of Japan, which he felt so deeply, really de-
mand his death? He glanced down at some wildflowers
near his feet and thought they will be alive tomorrow
and I will be dead. A humble weed would have more sig-
nificance than his life.

Nagatsuka took off along with six other suicide

The American aircraft carrier *Bunker Hill* was hit by two kamikaze planes in the sea off Okinawa on May 11, 1945; 396 crewmen were killed.

pilots. Alone in his cockpit he tried to sort out his thoughts. "Fear plagues me. I ask myself: 'Will I suffer at the moment of the explosion?'" He grasped the control column to steer his plane and stay in formation with his fellow kamikazes. "Suddenly a feeling of terrifying solitude freezes my blood. Who is my companion at the last moment? A soulless metal object—the control column! My body will be shattered to pieces and my right hand will hold fast to this companion in misfortune."[7]

Still many miles from Okinawa Nagatsuka entered a thick fog bank. Rain pelted his plane. The flight officer suddenly flew in front of him. Kamikaze airplanes carried no radios, but clearly the officer was pointing backwards, ordering him to return to the base. Why? Nagatsuka concluded it had to be because of the miserable weather. In the rain and fog the flight officer determined the squadron would never find the American ships. Nagatsuka turned back, depressed because now he would have to face the agony of certain death again. But because of Japan's chronic fuel shortage, the war ended before he was assigned another suicide mission. Nagatsuka survived the war and later wrote about his experiences in a book called *I Was A Kamikaze.*

In the waters off Okinawa the kamikazes raised havoc with the American fleet. The determined suicide pilots slipped through the swarms of fighter planes that protected American ships. They roared recklessly into hails of anti-aircraft fire. Thirty-four ships were sunk by the divine wind flyers and 368 were damaged. American sailors were forced to man their battle stations day and

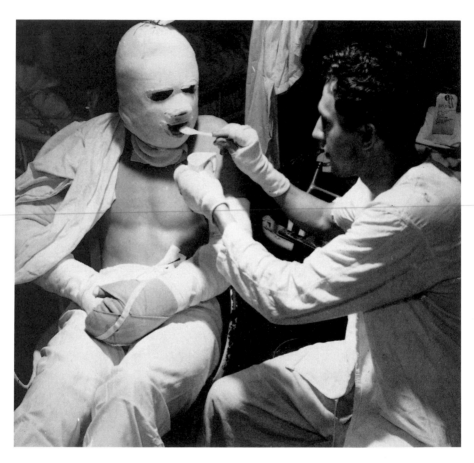

A sailor badly burned after his ship, the U.S.S. *Solace,* was hit by a kamikaze aircraft near Okinawa.

night, never knowing when a suicide pilot would come thundering down on their vessel. Nerves shattered and brave men went crazy from the strain. No American navy man would ever forget the kamikaze terror.

The Atomic Bomb

On the morning of April 12, 1945, President Roosevelt was working at his desk. Suddenly he said, "I have a terrific headache," then collapsed in his chair. He died a few hours later. Leadership of the nation passed to Harry S. Truman. It was only after Roosevelt's death that now-President Truman learned of the Manhattan Project, a massive effort by American and Allied scientists to develop an atomic bomb.

The Manhattan Project was the most ambitious scientific program ever undertaken by the United States. The nation spent two billion dollars on the effort, and the project employed 100,000 people who worked in 37 installations spread out over 13 states. Secrecy was such a vital concern that only a handful of the project's employees were aware they were making an atomic weapon. Not even Harry Truman, as vice president, knew America was building an atomic bomb.

In the New Mexico desert on July 16, 1945, a group of Manhattan Project scientists waited in a bunker to observe the first test explosion of the revolutionary new weapon. A voice over the bunker's loudspeaker droned a countdown, "three . . . two . . . one . . . " Then an incredible ball of fire burst out of the desert darkness. "[It was] the brightest light I have ever seen or I think anyone

Harry Truman became president after Roosevelt's death. As president
he made the momentous decision to drop the atomic bomb on Japan.

has ever seen," said one scientist. Inside the fireball temperatures were higher than on the surface of the sun. Desert sand underneath the blast melted and fused into glass. One of the inventors of the bomb, Dr. J. Robert Oppenheimer, quoted a line from ancient Hindu scripture, "I am become death, the shatterer of worlds."

After the successful test the decision to employ the new bomb rested with President Truman. A group of Manhattan Project scientists claimed it was too terrible a weapon to use, especially against Japan, a nation that seemed so close to defeat. Germany had surrendered on May 7, 1945, and the German collapse allowed the Allies to begin concentrating their naval and air might against the Japanese. The island nation of Japan was virtually surrounded by American ships, which cut off vital shipments of food and raw materials. But military leaders pointed out how savagely the Japanese fought for Iwo Jima and Okinawa, two of their last outposts in the Pacific. The generals and admirals estimated that an invasion of Japan would cost America one million killed and wounded. Truman ordered the atomic bomb to be dropped on a Japanese city as soon as possible.

Before dawn on August 6, 1945, a B-29 nicknamed the *Enola Gay* rumbled off an airfield at Tinian Island in the Marianas. In its bomb bay was a single whale-shaped bomb weighing 9,000 pounds. The *Enola Gay*'s pilot, Colonel Paul W. Tibbets, was informed by a scout plane that there was little cloud cover over the city of Hiroshima. The silvery B-29 arrived at that city and

A mushroom shaped cloud of smoke rises more than 60,000 feet into the sky over Nagasaki, Japan on August 8, 1945

dropped its bomb at 8:15 A.M. when Hiroshima's streets were crowded with men and women taking the streetcars to work and children running to school.

"Suddenly a glaring whitish-pink light appeared in the sky," wrote a Japanese journalist. "Within a few seconds the thousands of people in the streets . . . were scorched by a wave of searing heat. Many were killed instantly, others lay writhing on the ground screaming in agony from the intolerable pain of their burns. Everything standing upright in the way of the blast, walls, houses, factories, and other buildings, was annihilated; and the debris spun round in a whirlwind and was carried up in the air. Streetcars were picked up and tossed aside. . . . Trains were flung off the track as if they were toys."[8]

No one knows for sure, but it is believed 80,000 people were killed in Hiroshima by the atomic blast on that first day. Japanese leaders sank into a state of shock over the calamity. Three days later another B 29 dropped a second bomb this time on Nagasaki. In a radio message President Truman warned the Japanese to end the war or, "they may expect a rain of death from the air, the like of which has never been seen on earth."

On August 14, 1945, the Japanese government surrendered unconditionally to the United States. For months arguments had raged in Japanese government circles between those who wanted to sue for peace and those who demanded Japan fight on to the last man and woman. The atomic bomb and Russia's declaring war on

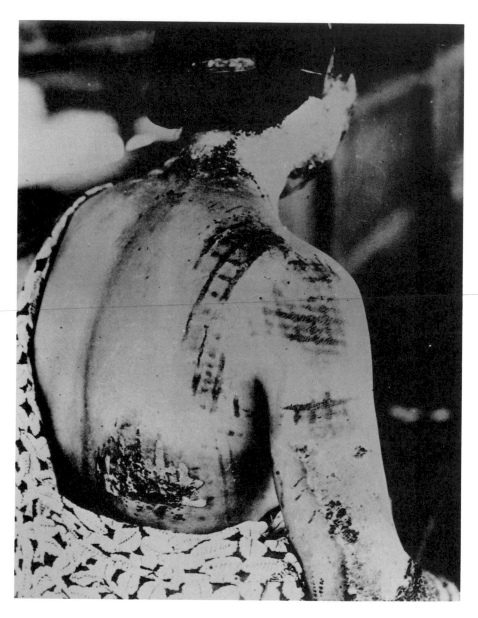

An atomic bomb victim with the pattern of her kimono burned into her back.

Japan on August 8 provided the last argument for the government leaders desiring peace. Japanese Emperor Hirohito, who the people regarded as a god, spoke on radio for the first time ever and urged his countrymen to "bear the unbearable," and accept defeat.

At long last World War II was over.

The guns were silenced. The war was over . . .
—President Harry S. Truman.

7 The Aftermath

On August 15, 1945, bedlam reigned in the United States as the nation celebrated final victory. Crowds poured onto city streets. Total strangers kissed each other. Church bells rang. Children formed parades and beat on garbage can covers. But in the wreckage that was Japan a stunned silence prevailed. Almost two million soldiers and seamen had been killed during the long years of war. Japan's industrial cities were burned-out shells. And the people had to face the ultimate humiliation of military occupation by the hated Americans.

In the early morning of August 28, 1945, a C-47 transport plane landed at an air base near Tokyo and taxied

A New York City neighborhood celebrates the Japanese surrender which ended World War II.

to a stop. Out stepped an army colonel named Charles Tench, a member of General Douglas MacArthur's staff. He was the first conqueror in history to set foot on Japanese soil. The details of this landing had been arranged by radio with the Japanese government, but Tench and his men feared being attacked by Bushido diehards. The Americans' worries proved groundless. The government had ordered the people to accept the American occupation. The Japanese, obedient in war, remained obedient in peace. Within 48 hours, hundreds of American troops landed at the airfield and were greeted stiffly, but politely by their one-time enemies.

On September 2, 1945, the official surrender ceremony was held on the battleship U.S.S. *Missouri*, docked in Tokyo Bay. After Japanese representatives signed the surrender document, General MacArthur, now the Supreme Commander for the Allied powers, made a speech, "It is my earnest hope—indeed the hope of all mankind—that from this solemn occasion a better world shall emerge out of the blood and carnage of the past, a world founded upon faith and understanding, a world dedicated to the dignity of man and the fulfillment of his most cherished wish for freedom, tolerance, and justice."

General MacArthur remained in Japan until 1951 and served as the military governor of that country. His power was so great that, in effect, he was America's viceroy over Japan. MacArthur was known for his conservative political views, but his administration of Japan was surprisingly liberal. He encouraged a strong labor movement. He broke up large land holdings and secured land for small farmers, and he helped to write a constitution fostering democracy and renouncing war. The most profound reform MacArthur demanded of Japan was to raise the status of women. Before the war women could not vote or hold political office, and they had little control over their lives. MacArthur insisted voting privileges be extended to women, and he eased restrictions on female ownership of business and land. One of MacArthur's advisers told him that Japanese men would be insulted by the sudden elevation of women to an equal status. "I don't care," MacArthur said. "I want to discredit the military. Women don't want war."

Grim faced Japanese prisoners of war, held in a compound on the island of Guam, hear the almost unbelievable news that Japan has agreed to surrender to the United States.

As a result of peace treaties, Japan surrendered its captured territories to the old colonial powers. Seven of the nation's warlords, including Hideki Tojo, were executed for committing war crimes. Russia gained land and considerable influence in Asia. Lost territories were restored to China, but the situation remained unstable there. During World War II the Chinese people fought three wars: the republican government fought the Communists, and both the republicans and the communists fought the Japanese. The end of the war against Japan then saw a civil war explode in China. The Chinese

General Douglas MacArthur signing the official surrender document on board the U.S.S. *Missouri* on September 2, 1945.

Prime Minister Hideki Tojo was one of seven Japanese warlords who were executed for war crimes.

communists under Mao Zedong triumphed, and China became a Communist nation in 1949.

The American occupation of Japan lasted for four years. In that time, a surprising bond developed between Americans and Japanese. The two peoples, who had harbored an insane hatred for each other in war, became friends in peace. The Japanese benefited from the friendship because they learned production techniques used by American factories. Armed with this knowledge, Japan became the richest country in Asia by the 1950s, and eventually it blossomed into an industrial powerhouse.

The conclusion of the Pacific War ended World War II, the most costly conflict in history. It is impossible to count the number of people who lost their lives during the war years. The war's final act—the bombing of Hiroshima and Nagasaki—put the world under the threat of nuclear extinction. No doubt many war veterans present during the surrender ceremony on the *Missouri* mused about the future as General MacArthur ended his speech with: "Let us pray that peace be now restored to the world, and that God will preserve it always. These proceedings are closed."

Chronology

September 18, 1931—Japan invades Manchuria, a region of China. The invasion was ordered by the warlords, a group of military officers and aggressive politicians who rose to the power in Japan during the 1930's. Some historians consider the invasion of Manchuria to be the actual start of World War II.

July 7, 1937—Shots are exchanged between Japanese and Chinese troops at the Marco Polo Bridge near the present-day city of Beijing in China. The Japanese warlords use the Marco Polo Bridge incident as a pretext to launch an undeclared war against China.

September 22, 1940—Japan invades French Indochina.

December 7, 1941—Japan launches a surprise air raid on the U.S. Navy base at Pearl Harbor in Hawaii. Only hours after the raid, Japanese planes bomb Singapore and Hong Kong, both British possessions.

December 10, 1941—The American defenders on the island of Guam surrender to the Japanese.

December 23, 1941—Japanese troops conquer the American outpost of Wake Island.

December 25, 1941—Hong Kong falls to the Japanese

January 2, 1942—Manila, the capital of the Philippines, surrenders to the Japanese army.

February 15, 1942—The British army defending Singapore surrenders.

April 9, 1942—The American force defending the Bataan Peninsula in the Philippines surrenders.

April 19, 1942—American bombers launched from the aircraft carrier U.S.S. *Hornet*, complete the first air raid on Japan.

May 4 to May 8, 1942—The Japanese and the American navies each lose one aircraft carrier at the Battle of the Coral Sea, the first naval battle in history fought exclusively by carrier planes.

June 3 to June 6, 1942—At the Battle of Midway, the Japanese navy suffers the loss of four of its finest aircraft carriers; the battle is the major turning point in the Pacific War.

August 7, 1942—American marines land at Guadalcanal island; the assault marks the first major offensive thrust by the United States against Japan.

November 1, 1942—U.S. troops invade Bougainville, an island near Guadalcanal; this invasion begins an "island hopping" campaign designed to bring island bases ever closer to Japanese shores.

November 20, 1943—American marines assault Tarawa, and begin one of the bloodiest island battles of the war.

January 31, 1944—American soldiers storm the island of Kwajalein.

June 15, 1944—Marines hit the beach at Saipan Island in the Marianas chain.

June 15, 1944—The new and powerful B-29 bomber raids Japan for the first time.

October 20, 1944—Americans land at island of Leyte in

the Philippines; General Douglas MacArthur fulfills his pledge: "I shall return."

October 23 to October 26—The Japanese navy loses three battleships, four carriers, and ten cruisers at the Battle of Leyte Gulf.

January 9, 1945—American and Filipino troops invade Luzon, the Philippines' main island.

February 19, 1945—Marines land on Iwo Jima.

March 10, 1945—The first massive air raid using B-29 bombers is launched against Tokyo.

April 1, 1945—Soldiers and marines attack Okinawa, an island 450 miles from mainland Japan; the Japanese fight back by sending waves of kamikaze planes to disrupt the invasion fleet.

May 7, 1945—Germany surrenders allowing the Allies to begin transferring their troops, ships and planes to the Pacific theater.

July 16, 1945 The atomic bomb is test-fired at a secret site in the New Mexico desert.

August 6, 1945—A B-29 drops a single atomic bomb on Hiroshima; at least 80,000 people were killed by the blast.

August 8, 1945—Russia declares war on Japan.

August 9, 1945—An atomic bomb is dropped on Nagasaki.

August 14, 1945—Japan surrenders to the Allies.

September 2, 1945—The official surrender documents are signed in a ceremony on board the U.S.S. *Missouri,* docked in Tokyo Bay.

Notes by Chapter

Chapter 1

1. Robert LaForte and Ronald Marcello, *Remembering Pearl Harbor, Eyewitness Accounts of U.S. Military Men and Women* (Wilmington, Delaware, Scholarly Resources, Inc., 1991), p. 42.

2. Ibid., p. 43.

3. Ibid., p. 19.

Chapter 2

1. Franklin D. Roosevelt, "Quarantine the Aggressors"; speech delivered in Chicago, 1937. Reprinted from *Annals of America,* vol. 15, p. 504.

2. Winston Churchill, *The Second World War*, Vol. 3, *The Grand Alliance* (Boston, Houghton, Mifflin Company, 1950), p. 520.

3. W. Scott Cunningham, *Wake Island Command* (Boston, Little, Brown and Company, 1961), p. 113.

4. Dick Bilyeu, *Lost in Action: A World War II Soldier's Account of Capture on Bataan and Imprisonment by the Japanese* (London, England, McFarland & Company, Inc., 1991), p. 77.

Chapter 3

1. Ted Lawson, *Thirty Seconds Over Tokyo* (New York, Random House, 1943), pp. 55–56.

2. *Life* Magazine, June 1, 1942.

3. Samuel Eliot Morison, *The Two-Ocean War* (Boston, Little, Brown and Company, 1963), p. 162.

4. Richard Tregaskis, *Guadalcanal Diary* (New York, Random House, 1943) p. 47.

5. Editors, *Yank* (Army weekly), *Yank, The Story of World War II as Written by Its Soldiers* (New York, Greenwich House, 1984), p. 195.

Chapter 4

1. Roger Manvell, *Films and the Second World War* (South Brunswick and New York, A. S. Barnes and Company, 1974), p. 188.

2. Studs Terkel, *The Good War* (New York, Pantheon Books, 1984), p. 237.

3. Yoshiko Uchida, *Desert Exile: The Uprooting of a Japanese American Family* (Seattle, Washington, The University of Washington Press, 1982), p. 67.

4. Roy Hoopes, *Americans Remember the Home Front* (New York, Hawthorn Books, 1977), p. 183.

5. Terkel, p. 228.

6. Terkel, p. 227.

7. Mikiso Hane, *Peasants, Rebels, and Outcasts: The Underside of Modern Japan* (New York: Pantheon Books, 1982), p. 239.

Chapter 5

1. Hughston E. Lowder, *Batfish: The Champion "Submarine-Killer" of World War II* (Englewood Cliffs, New Jersey, Prentice-Hall, Inc., 1980), p. 109.

2. *Time* Magazine, December 27, 1943.

3. *The New Yorker Book of War Pieces* (New York, Schocken Books, 1947), pp. 410–411.

Chapter 6

1. General Curtis E. LeMay, *Superfortress, The B-29 and American Airpower* (New York, McGraw-Hill, Inc., 1988), p. 123.

2. Robert Guillain, *I Saw Tokyo Burning* (New York, Doubleday & Company, 1981), p. 184.

3. *The New Yorker Book of War Pieces* (New York, Schocken Books, 1947), p. 466.

4. William Manchester, *Goodbye Darkness: A Memoir of the Pacific War* (Boston, Little, Brown and Company, 1979), p. 360.

5. Ibid., p. 382.

6. Ryuji Nagatsuka, *I Was a Kamikaze* (New York, Macmillan, 1972), p. 181.

7. Ibid., p. 189.

8. C. L. Sulzberger, *The American Heritage History of World War II* (eyewitness accounts section), (New York, American Heritage Publishing Company, 1966), p. 617.

Further Reading

Black, Wallace and Blashfield, Jean F. *Island Hopping in the Pacific.* New York: Macmillan. 1992.

Black, Wallace and Blashfield, Jean F. *Guadalcanal.* New York: Macmillan. 1992.

Bliven, Bruce. *From Pearl Harbor to Okinawa: The War in the Pacific, 1941-1945.* New York: Random House, 1960.

Davis, Daniel. *Behind Barbed Wire; The Imprisonment of Japanese Americans in World War II.* New York: E.P. Dutton, 1982.

DeJong, Meindert. *The House of Sixty Fathers.* New York: Harper, 1956. (A work of fiction)

Humble, Richard. *World War II Aircraft Carrier.* New York: Franklin Watts, 1989.

Leckie, Robert. *Battle for Iwo Jima.* New York: Random House, 1967.

Marrin, Albert. *Victory in the Pacific.* New York: Athenium, 1983.

Maruki, Toshi. *Hiroshima No Pika.* New York: Lothrop, 1982.

McGowan, Tom. *Midway and Guadalcanal.* New York: Franklin Watts, 1984.

Mercer, Charles. *Miracle at Midway.* New York: Putnam's, 1977.

Sears, Stephen. *Carrier War in the Pacific.* New York: Harper and Row, 1966.

Stein, R. Conrad. *The Home Front.* Chicago: Childrens Press, 1986.

Stein, R. Conrad. *Hiroshima.* Chicago: Childrens Press, 1987.

Tregaskis, Richard. *Guadalcanal Diary.* New York: Random House, 1943.

Index

About the Author

R. Conrad Stein was born and raised in Chicago. He served in the U.S. Marine Corps in the mid-1950's, when the United States was at peace. After being discharged from the marines he attended the University of Illinois where he received a degree in history. Mr. Stein later earned an advanced degree from the University of Guanajuato in Mexico. The author lives in Chicago with his wife, Deborah Kent, who is also an author of books for young readers. They have a daughter, Janna.

The study of history is Mr. Stein's hobby. He thinks of the past as a special and very exciting world. Mr. Stein has written more than fifty history books for young readers.